HUMAN COMMUNICATION HANDBOOK
Simulations and Games

HUMAN COMMUNICATION HANDBOOK
Simulations and Games

Brent D. Ruben, Ph.D.
Director, Institute of Communication Studies
Rutgers University
New Jersey

Richard W. Budd, Ph.D.
Chairman, Department of Human Communication
Rutgers University
New Jersey

HAYDEN BOOK COMPANY, INC.
Rochelle Park, New Jersey

Library of Congress Cataloging in Publication Data

Ruben, Brent D
  Human communication handbook.

  Includes bibliographies.
  1. Interpersonal relations. 2. Communication--
Social aspects. 3. Communication--Psychological
aspects. I. Budd, Richard W., joint author.
II. Title.
HM132.R82   301.14   74-23696
ISBN 0-8104-5524-2

Printed in the United States of America

1 2 3 4 5 6 7 8 9   PRINTING

75 76 77 78 79 80 81 82   YEAR

Preface

Becoming truly competent in communication—in communicating—to and being communicated with—requires a unique combination of theoretical understanding and practical skill. Neither alone is sufficient. This book is intended to provide the basic ingredients for achieving this delicate integration.

Human Communication Handbook: Simulations and Games provides a basic framework for conceiving of human communication, and a collection of carefully selected and ordered experience-based learning activities designed to bring the framework to life for the learner. Through participation in a variety of simulations, games, and structured exercises in conjunction with careful observation and class discussion, students can learn firsthand the dynamics of intrapersonal, small group, organizational, and mass communication.

Because of the vast and ever-changing nature of human communication processes, this book is not intended to provide its users with ultimate "right" answers about how effective or successful communication can be accomplished in *all* situations. No one knows that, nor is anyone ever likely to! The activities are designed therefore to foster an increased awareness of how communication works, and the part each of us personally plays in the outcomes.

New Brunswick, New Jersey

BRENT RUBEN
RICHARD BUDD

Acknowledgments

To the many persons whose ideas have contributed to our thinking about human communication, experience-based learning, and education, and to those innumerable individuals who have helped in the development and elaboration of the activities in this volume, we offer our sincere appreciation. We have tried to justly acknowledge these efforts throughout this book.

We particularly wish to express our thanks for the contributions of Marjorie W. Longley, Manager of Educational Marketing and Development of *The New York Times*. Her encouragement and vitality were instrumental to the development of these materials. We would also like to express our appreciation to Kyle Kurtz and Jann Ruben for their continuing commitment to this project. In many respects, this volume reflects as much their contribution as ours. Special thanks also to Kathi Teichman, Barbara Duska, and Dianne Littwin, each of whom provided a critical ingredient necessary to the completion of this book.

B. R.
R. B.

Credits

The Authors wish to express their appreciation for permission to include the following materials in this book:

Games 6, 15, 16, 18, 23, 42, and 44: Developed by Lanie Melamed, Dawson College, McGill University, Montreal, Quebec.

Game 13: Adapted with permission from Haney, *Communication and Organizational Behavior,* (rev. Ed.); Homewood, Ill.: Richard D. Irwin, Inc.

Games 17, 19, 28, 31, and 40: Adapted from an exercise developed at the University of Iowa, Title IV Institute on Problems of Classroom Desegregation, Iowa City, Iowa.

Game 22: Adapted from H. J. Leavitt, *Managerial Psychology,* 1st Ed.; © 1958, The University of Chicago Press, pp. 121-122.

Game 24: Adapted from "Learning about Behavior Styles," National Training Laboratories, 1970.

Game 29: This exercise is adapted from *Communication Patterns in Task Oriented Groups,* by Alex Bavelas, from which "Hollow Square: A Communication Experiment" was adapted in *A Handbook of Structural Experiences for Human Relations,* Vol. II, J. W. Pfeiffer and J. E. Jones (Eds.). San Diego: University Associates, 1972. Reprinted by permission of University Associates.

Fig. 34.1: Adapted from *Handbook of Staff Development and Human Relations Training:* Materials developed for use in Africa, by Donald Nylen, J. Robert Mitchell, and Anthony Stout. National Training Laboratories.

Fig. 34.2: The statements used in this exercise are based upon items developed by Todd T. Hunt of the Department of Human Communication, Rutgers University.

Fig. 34.4: Adapted from Appendix 1, *Encounter Groups:* First Facts, by Morton A. Lieberman, Irvin D. Yalom, and Matthew B. Miles, © 1973 by Morton A. Lieberman, Irvin D. Yalom and Matthew B. Miles, Basic Books, Inc., Publishers, New York.

Game 38: Adapted from a game developed by Barbara Aikins, University of Iowa, 1969.

Game 39: Adapted from material developed by Marjorie Longley, *Educational Marketing,* The New York Times, © 1972 by The New York Times. Reprinted by permission.

Game 41: Adapted from the game of *Power,* created by Arthur and Wald Amberstone. The rules of *Power* and any additional information can be obtained by writing to the Great Game and Symbol Company, Westminster Road, Brooklyn, N.Y. 11218.

Game 43: Designed by Pri and Chris Notowidigdo, Limbour, Quebec.

Game 45: *Hypothetica* was developed by Richard W. Budd, Department of Human Communication, Rutgers University, in 1965, and used extensively by the Agency for International Development in Communication Seminars, administered by Michigan State University Department of Communication.

Game 46: Adapted from "T Building: Communication and Society" by Joseph Ascroft and John Cipolla.

Game 47: Developed by Henry G. LaBrie III and Brent D. Ruben. Originally published in unedited form in *Communication: Journalism Education Today,* Fall, 1972.

Game 48: Adapted from "The Classroom Pressbox" by Henry G. LaBrie III and Brent D. Ruben, Institute for Communication Studies, University of Iowa, 1971.

Game 49: Adapted from "Communication System Simulation" by Albert D. Talbott and Brent D. Ruben, School of Journalism, University of Iowa, Iowa City, Iowa, 1970. A revised, detailed version is provided in *Interact* by Brent D. Ruben, Kennebunkport, Maine: Mercer House Press, 1973.

Guide 1: Adapted from K. Benne and P. Sheats, "Functional Roles of Group Members," *Journal of Social Research,* Vol. 4, No. 2 (1948).

Guide 4: Adapted from "What to Look for in Groups: An Observation Guide" by Philip G. Hanson in *The 1972 Annual Handbook for Group Facilitators,* J. W. Pfeiffer and J. E. Jones (Eds.). San Diego: University Associates, 1972. Reprinted by permission of University Associates.

Guides 6 and 8: Alice Miel, "A Group Studies Itself to Improve Itself," *Teachers College Record,* Vol. 49, No. 1, October 1947, pp. 31-43.

Guide 11: Adapted from "Feedback and the Helping Relationship": Reading Book 1967, National Training Laboratories.

Contents

Human Communication: An Overview **1**

References **9**

Bibliography **11**

PART 1 — Personal Communication **19**
    1. Self-Disclosure and Listening *21*
    2. Self Perception and Value Orientation *22*
    3. Seeing and Not Seeing *24*
    4. Closure *28*
    5. Experience and Language *30*
    6. Environmental Awareness *32*
    7. Categorization *33*
    8. Perceptual Context *36*
    9. Object Awareness *39*
    10. Perceptual Set *40*
    11. Learning and Change *41*
    12. Assumptions *45*
    13. Observations and Inferences *46*
    14. Predicting Attitudes *49*
    15. Silence *50*
    16. Personal Space *51*
    17. Paralanguage *53*
    18. Eye Contact Patterns *54*
    19. Situational Geography *55*
    20. Kinesics *56*
    Bibliography 58

PART 2 — Social Communication **61**
    21. Rumor: Serial Transmission of Information *62*
    22. Feedback *64*
    23. Prediction and Interpersonal Perception *68*
    24. Behavior Differences *69*

25. Group-to-One Feedback *70*
26. Group Formation *71*
27. Grouping *72*
28. Communicator Credibility *73*
29. Cooperative and Competitive Communication *74*
30. Trust *76*
31. Minority and Majority Communication *79*
32. Group Problem-Solving *80*
33. Group Initiation and Membership *81*
34. Group Decision Making *82*
35. Leadership *86*
    Bibliography 88

PART 3 – Communication Systems **93**
36. Intergroup Organization *95*
37. Task Planning and Intergroup Coordination *97*
38. Conflict, Confrontation, and Conflict Resolution *103*
39. Mass Communication and Community
    Decision-Making *106*
40. Communication and Intra-Community
    Problem-Solving *109*
41. Society, Communication and Power *113*
42. Cross Cultural Communication:
    Introductions and Departures *115*
43. Cross Cultural Awareness and Stereotyping *117*
44. Time, Timing, and Culture *120*
45. Communication and Development – Hypothetica:
    A Social Action Game *121*
46. Communication and Social Integration *132*
47. Political Communication *135*
48. Mass Communication and the Pressbox *138*
49. Communication System Simulation *139*
    Bibliography 145

PART 4 – Communication Observation and Recording Guides 151
1. Descriptions of Common Roles in Interpersonal
   and Group Communication *153*
2. Role Behavior Recording Form *155*
3. Interpersonal and Small Group Role
   Description Form *156*
4. Group Communication Observation Form *157*

5. Recording Information Networks *160*
6. Small Group Interaction Content Guide *161*
7. Intra-Group Perception Guide *162*
8. Verbal Interaction Recording Guide *164*
9. Seating Arrangement Recording Guide *166*
10. Interpersonal Communication Observation Form *168*
11. Guidelines for Providing Useful Feedback *169*
12. Barriers to Communication *170*
13. Intra-Group Evaluation Form *171*
14. Group Climate Inventory *172*
15. Personal and Group Meeting Reaction Form *173*
16. Individual and Group Climate Guide *174*

HUMAN COMMUNICATION HANDBOOK
Simulations and Games

HUMAN COMMUNICATION: An Overview

Human communication is that fundamental life process through which we sense, make sense of, and transact with our environment and the people in it. Other than the metabolic processes through which we process matter for energy, we have no means of influencing or of being influenced by our environment except through communication.

This particular statement about the process of human communication seems straightforward enough. Why, then, do most people find it difficult to conceive of communication in these terms, and even more difficult to integrate and reflect such an understanding in their day-to-day behavior? Perhaps one major reason is that most of us already think we know what communication means. After all, most of us have been doing it for a number of years now, and we seem to have survived.

For many, communication is synonymous with talking and writing—in effect, language. Accordingly, if people would only speak more plainly and write with more clarity, most of our communication problems would disappear. Others hold communication in greater awe, believing it to be something done by professionals in the media—radio, television, magazines—rather than by individuals in their everyday lives. The point is, what people *think* communication is becomes considerably less important than how that understanding is reflected in their *behavior*. The strongest position for understanding the phenomenon is, of course, possessing a conceptual framework about communication that is internally consistent with the way one behaves.

What seems to derive from the foregoing discussion is, at the least, two different perspectives for approaching communication education: 1. the development of ways of thinking and talking about the phenomenon; 2. the creation of a learning environment in which the thinking and learning grow from direct experiences in the doing. Clearly these two approaches are by no means mutually exclusive, but operationally they do seem to delineate distinct ways in which courses and curricula are currently designed and taught.

The position assumed in this handbook is that the two pedagogical approaches are mutually strengthened when they are blended together in a single program. One without the other, we believe, can lead to a sterile educational experience for instructor and learner alike. Learning to think and talk about content—facts, theories, sequences, rules, etc.—can lead to verbal glibness which frequently cannot be translated into action. Learning only from experience can turn the educational experience into an undisciplined playground from which the student learns precious little about conceptualization and the power of generalization. Together, the two methodologies embroil the student in a strong interaction of intellectual learning and testing their learning through experience.

Throughout its history, the primary emphasis in education has been placed upon the intellectual learning of content. And while the conceptual roots of experience-based learning date to the works of John Dewey [1] and Maria Montessori,[2] writing nearly three-quarters of a century ago, it has only been in recent years that educators have paid any real attention to its potential. For these reasons, the main thrust of this book is toward the experience-based approach, although carefully constructed bibliographies of appropriate theoretical materials follow each section.

A major contributor to rekindling interest in "learning by doing" has come from the business and industrial community where in the past several decades an increased emphasis has been placed upon organizational development, human relations, internal communication, and employee and management in-service training, in general. In searching for training techniques which seemed theoretically sound and operationally compelling, games, simulations, role playing activities and structured exercises were adopted.

Social psychologists, sociologists and individuals in the fields of communication and management provided another influence as a consequence of their study of group dynamics, leadership and group decision-making. Experiential learning found growing acceptance also with psychiatrists, social workers, counselors, religious leaders and others who applied the techniques in therapeutic training contexts.

An additional source of influence came directly from work in the area of games and simulations. As Tansey and Unwin [3] note, the use of simulation and games has a lengthy heritage, dating perhaps to the development of chess as a symbolic tactical encounter between opposing factions. War games of various sorts were also used widely in World War II, particularly by the Japanese and Germans and later by the United States and Soviet Union.[4]

Perhaps the single greatest thrust has come as a result of a broadly-based questioning of traditional educational values, systems of instruction and approaches to learning. The scholarly contributions of Bruner [5] and Rogers [6] have had a particular impact in this regard, along with the more popular works of such individuals as Postman and Weingartner,[7] Riesman,[8] Goodman [9] and Holt,[10] to mention only a few. The following passage from the student-authored *Champaign Report* provides a succinct statement of some of the underlying concerns which have since been more broadly voiced:

The artificial gulf between ideas and action must be bridged so that learners learn ideas for action.

Faculty members ought to try taking a student to lunch sometime.

Smallness or largeness have no inherent value in an institution, but continued opportunity for contact with diverse primary groups must be offered to all students.

Efficiency has been overrated as an educational device, and chaos has been underrated.

We must develop devices for continued examination of what is significant and what is insignificant learning.

Base learning on problem solving. Get a bunch of freshmen together and tell them: We have a problem and we want you to work on it for the next four years. How do you feed the world? At the end of that time, you'll have sociologists and botanists and engineers and political scientists, and God knows what, but they will have learned because they had an important question to answer and because they thought their particular discipline might shed some light on it.[11]

In response to these and other suggestions, experience-based learning has been perceived as one potent means of rejuvenating, restyling, or complementing the standard classroom learning environment.

Nourished by these and other influences, experiential learning has continued to grow in popularity and acceptance. And as has been noted often in the literature, experience-based learning, at face value at least, has numerous advantages over alternative instructional methods. For one thing, simulations and games are generally constructed with a problem focus and participants frequently seem well motivated as a consequence. Experience-based learning, it has been said, fosters questioning, inquiry and structural learning in addition to teaching specific content. Another frequently mentioned virtue of experiential settings is the capability for minimizing space and time constraints often present in alternative training contexts; students need not wait days, months or years to gain a sense of the consequences of their decisions and actions. Experience-based environments also seem to be particularly useful for helping students come to understand and learn to cope directly with *change* and ambiguity. And, of course, in a laboratory environment, risks, responsibilities and severity of outcomes can be controlled to make it possible for participants to "fail" without full consequence.

In the excitement created by student enthusiasm for and involvement in simulation and games, we may have a tendency to forget that the designer of such activities faces the same problems and issues that have plagued the traditional educator for years. Simulation and games are, after all, simply another form of instruction, and both the design and execution of any simulation will necessarily be constrained by and reflect the educational philosophy of its designers and users. The point is that any use of the experience-based learning format must be imbedded in the context of a more general program which focuses on some set of educational objectives. The stringing together of the exercises detailed in this book will not, in and of themselves, meet that end.

Ultimately, of course, as educators we must deal with the prospect that what the instructor has in mind when he designs a learning environment may have little or nothing to do with how the student understands that same situation. The designer may very well intend the simulation or game to give rise to certain kinds of problems and questions which he feels will be beneficial for students to cope with. But in creating that activity for himself, the student may very well define the environment and the problems quite differently from the way the designer did. In short, the outcomes an instructor hopes for in using a certain exercise might simply not come to pass. It is at this crucial juncture that the question of the validity of employing experience-based learning exercises is most frequently raised. Interestingly enough, the problems of coping with a simulation or game which goes "awry" are not the students' problems (because they did it wrong), but the instructor's (if he fails to take advantage of the learning that has occurred). How any educator handles this particular problem, obviously, depends upon the philosophical framework from which he or she is operating.

For the educator who defines his goal primarily as passing along accumulated knowledge and experience, and who has set out to demonstrate how a particular theory or set of communication principles operates, an exercise that turns out differently than intended must be viewed as a failure. In dealing with this problem, the instructor must carefully note the points at which deviations occur. The corrective measures normally called for in such a situation are adding parameters or making changes in sequencing to reduce the ambiguity of the environment, so as to ensure that participants operate in ways consistent with the theory being taught. Exercises of this nature are perhaps more properly referred to as demonstrative rather than experience-based.

On the other hand, as an instructor becomes more familiar with the use of experience-based exercises, and can come to define their use as providing a context in which students can communicate and be communicated-with, he may welcome these deviations as an opportunity to underscore the personal nature of communication and the range of understandings that, as a result, are bound to evolve. From this view, the primary concern will be that students learn about their own communication behavior and the manner in which they affect and are affected by others. This sort of outcome from an exercise always occurs, whether the simulation or game goes according to plan or not.

This is not to say that using experience-based exercises from this broader perspective eliminates all of the instructional problems; it simply generates a much different set of them. In deciding to use even the most open, rule-free exercise, the instructor obviously has some notion of what he anticipates from those who will participate. Without such speculation, he would be unable to set even the broadest parameters, and would not, in fact, have the slightest reason for using an experience-based exercise in the first place. And since these exercises for the most part will be used in educational institutions, we will assume that most educators would be concerned that their students be able to learn something, however diverse and however personal those learnings, from having participated in an exercise. The extent to which these factors influence the way the instructor manages the exercise are directly related to the "problems" he will have in managing it. In other words, simply employing a more open-ended design does not somehow automatically free the educator from falling victim to his own intentions for and anticipations of learning outcomes.

As the instructor, employing the experience-based activity, watches over whatever it is he has put into motion, it is quite easy to become seduced by the impression that what he intended or expected or only hoped would happen, seems not to be happening. He may feel the participants have organized themselves in a most inefficient manner, or that they are not attending to (perhaps not even identifying) problems that he sees cropping up here and there, or that the whole thing has simply collapsed into a confused and irretrievable debacle. In any case, the temptation to bring corrective measures to bear so the students cannot help but notice or name or deal with the problems with which the instructor is concerned can become great indeed. And while the recommended remedy for such conditions in a demonstration type exercise is to correct such error through the imposition of additional parameters, the same sort of intervention might well deal a crippling blow to a more open-ended exercise.

Error, diversity, ambiguity and even chaos are the lifeblood of an experience-based environment. They provide the raw data out of which each participant, through his own methods in his own way and in his time, must construct for himself patterns and theories and behaviors that permit him to successfully cope with the environment around him on the one hand, and move toward the goals he has defined for himself on the other. For the educator to intervene and attempt to control the directions of that struggle, even if he believes it destined for disastrous failure, is to deny the student the opportunity to deal with the consequences of his own behavior. No amount of telling the student about "correct" or "inappropriate" behaviors will help him better understand his own or the behavior of others. To understand better how he behaves, he must behave. Ultimately, such interventions shed more light on the educator's own concept of reality than they do upon what the students' behavior "mean."

Managing experience-based games and simulations is, at its best, a difficult and trying task. Such simulations are not designed to meet the instructor's needs to function as an "educator." Unlike the traditional classroom setting for demonstrations, where control of the environment rests squarely in the hands of the instructor, control in the experience-based environment is dispersed among the participants. The discomfort attending ambiguity becomes not only something that the participants must contend with, it necessarily engulfs the instructor in the environment as well. The painful difference is that the participants can act to relieve their anxiety; the instructor cannot. In addition, the instructor finds that the traditional standards of assessing the learning situation fail him. He must be content to believe that even inactivity and boredom also serve to teach. The instructor's knowledge of what was learned is limited since he has no viable way of measuring what learnings take place. He has not even been able to save his students from failure or to "grade them down" for failing, since failure (or at least the opportunity for failure) is seen as a necessary and positive component of the learning environment.

In sum, perhaps the greater chance for the "failure" of the process learning environment rests not with the students as they thrash around in seemingly unorthodox ways to bring order to ambiguity, but with the educator who finds himself unequal to the very task he is demanding of his students.

The Communication Framework

While we have discussed experience-based learning in terms of communication games and exercises, it might be useful to discuss briefly the framework underlying the organization of this book. We have opted not to make this section serve as a communication primer. We simply re-iterate our suggestion that the bibliographic materials accompanying each section of the book be referenced to provide the substance of courses in which these exercises are used. For our purposes, we have organized the content into three sections: Personal Communication, Social Communication, and Mass Communication and Communication Systems.

One useful way to think about what human communication is, focuses first upon the individual and the nature of personal communication. It is through personal communication that each individual transacts with his environment and, in so doing, attaches meaning and significance to the persons, things and events around him. This view implies a concern not only for how one *communicates-to* others, but also how one is *communicated-with*. Similarly it suggests that communication involves not only what an individual does, says or intends, but also with the whole range of intended and unintended consequences and significances which may be attached to his behavior by others. Conceived in this manner, it is clear that one's failure to speak may indeed have as much communicative consequence as the opposite. And if we leave out something from this section of discussion which a reader thought should have been included, our omission may communicate any one of a variety of things, none of which may bear any relationship to what we said or intended.

From this view of communication, the focus is upon both the initiator of messages—whether spoken, non-verbal, or written—and what he is attempting to do, as well as the listener or audience member and the meanings and significance which he may attach.

When the level of analysis shifts from the individual and personal communication, to the nature, intents, and consequences of the communicative relationship between two or more persons, the focus may be termed social communication. Whether in a classroom, a gathering of friends, a marriage, or a society, communication provides and maintains the links between people which make social organization and cooperation possible. It is, of course, through social communication (in one form or another) that we acquire most of our knowledge, attitudes, beliefs, values, and opinions of the present and past, and it is on this same basis that we come to develop ways to make predictions about the future.

Mass Communication evolves out of the interface of personal and social communication. It involves the production of messages, meanings, or environments by one or a few persons, for distribution to and influence upon a larger audience. Often mass communication has been thought of in terms only of public media—newspapers, radio, television, magazines, and occasionally books, films, and theatre. There is, however, a more general sense in which architecture, libraries, museums, highways, the fashion industry, and even restaurants fit the definition of mass communication institutions. They operate similarly and serve the same basic functions for humans as do the more traditionally defined public media.

Depending upon one's goals, the participants, and the demands of the situation, the exercises in this book may be used as the basis for a total program in human communication or as supplementary activities in other instructional or training programs. The exercises are suitable for use in sequential order or any other ordering which fits the instructional objectives of a particular situation.

The volume is designed so that generally, as one moves through the volume the exercises progress in complexity and sophistication. Activities in the early portion of the volume are generally designed to make rather specific points or direct attention to fundamental issues about human communication. They are more like demonstrations than simulations. As one moves to later activities the exercises are intended to allow for participants to have an increasing impact upon the directions and outcomes of activity, and the role of the instructor or facilitator shifts from information-giver to discussion leader and question raiser. These activities require a greater commitment by both participants and instructor.

In addition to the three sections of simulations and games, there is also a section providing an assortment of observation guides which are intended for use by participants and/or instructor to help identify and record communication dynamics which occur during any of the activities presented in the book.

Additional sections of the volume provide a selective bibliography of relevant references in human communication, experience-based learning, games, simulations, structured exercises, and other instructional techniques for communication training.

References

1. Readers interested in pursuing these notions in depth may wish to examine *John Dewey: Lectures in the Philosophy of Education, 1899* by Reginald D. Archambault (New York: Random House, 1966), especially Lectures VI and VII, pp. 59–75.

   On pages 65–66 of that volume Dewey says: "There seems a very practical existing tendency in the direction of the recognition of this principle, that fundamentally speaking, the educative process must be the same within and without the school walls. . . . When we say the materials and methods are the same it is not that all distinction must be wiped out or overlooked, but it does mean that the school has for its function the organization in a more conscious and thorough going way the resources and the methods and materials that are used in the more unconscious and haphazard way outside."

   See also John Dewey, *Experience and Education* (New York: Macmillan, 1938) and *Democracy and Education* (New York: The Free Press, 1916).
2. Readers interested in writings of Maria Montessori may wish to examine *The Montessori Method* (New York: Schocken Books, 1964) and *Spontaneous Activity in Education* (New York: Schocken Books, 1965).
3. P. J. Tansey and Derick Unwin, *Simulations and Gaming in Education* (London: Metheun Education, Ltd., 1969), p. 1.
4. John R. Raser, *Simulation and Society: An Exploration of Scientific Gaming* (Boston: Allyn and Bacon, 1969), p. 1.
5. See especially *The Relevance of Education,* J. S. Bruner (New York: W. W. Norton & Co., 1971); *Learning About Learning: A Conference Report*, J. S. Bruner (ed.) (Washington: U.S. Government Printing Office, 1966); J. S. Bruner, *The Process of Education* (Cambridge, Mass.: Harvard Press, 1961); J. S. Bruner, *Toward a Theory of Instruction* (New York: Norton, 1966); and J. S. Bruner, Rose R. Oliver and Patricia M. Greenfield, *et. al.*, Studies in *Cognitive Growth* (New York: John Wiley & Sons, 1966).
6. See especially *Encounter Groups,* Carl Rogers (New York: Harper and Row, 1970); "The Characteristics of a Helping Relationship," excerpted from *On Becoming a Person* by Carl Rogers (Boston: Houghton Mifflin, 1961), Chapter 3, pp. 39–58; Carl Rogers, *Freedom to Learn* (Columbus, Ohio: Charles E. Merrill Publishing Co., 1969); Carl Rogers, "Interpersonal Relationships: U.S.A. 2000." This paper was part of a symposium sponsored by the Esalen Institute, San Francisco, entitled "USA 2000" on January 10, 1968. See also Carl R. Rogers, "The Process of the Basic Encounter Group,"

in *Challenges of Humanistic Psychology,* James F. T. Bugental (ed.) (New York: McGraw-Hill, 1967).

7. Neil Postman and Charles Weingartner, *Teaching as a Subversive Activity* (New York: Delacorte Press, 1969).

8. Especially *Constraint and Variety in American Education,* David Riesman (Lincoln, Nebr.: University of Nebraska Press, 1968).

9. Especially *Compulsory Mis-education,* Paul Goodman (New York: Vintage Books, Random House, 1962).

10. Especially *How Children Learn,* John Holt (New York: Pitman Publishing Co., 1967).

11. *Champaign Report: A Conference on Educational Reform, A Student View,* Paul Danish (ed.) (Champaign, Ill.: September, 1966), pp. 6–7.

Bibliography

Communication Theory

Allport, Gordon W., *Becoming*, New Haven: Yale University Press, 1955.

Berger, Peter L., *The Sacred Canopy*, Garden City, N.Y.: Doubleday, 1969.

Berger, Peter L. and Thomas Luckman, *The Social Construction of Reality, A Treatise on the Sociology of Knowledge*, Garden City, N.Y.: Doubleday, 1966.

Blumer, Herbert, *Symbolic Interactionism*, Englewood Cliffs, N.J.: Prentice-Hall, 1969.

Bruner, J. S., *The Process of Education*, Cambridge, Mass.: Harvard Press, 1961.

Bruner, J. S., *Toward a Theory of Instruction*, New York: Norton, 1966.

Budd, Richard W. and Malcolm S. MacLean, Jr., "Applying Communication Principles to Communication Education," *Communication Spectrum '7*, Proceedings of the 1966 National Society for the Study of Communication Meeting, Denver, Colorado.

Budd, Richard W., "Communication, Education and Simulation, Some Thoughts on the Learning Process," Institute for Communication Studies, University of Iowa, 1970.

Budd, Richard W. and Brent D. Ruben, *Approaches to Human Communication*, New York: Spartan Books, 1972.

Budd, Richard W. and Brent D. Ruben, *Approaches to Mass Communication*, (in preparation).

Church, Joseph, *Language and the Discovery of Reality*, New York: Vintage Books, 1961,

Dewey, John, *Experience and Education*, New York: Collier Books, Collier-MacMillan, 1938, 1963.

Duncan, Hugh Dalziel, *Communication and Social Order*, London: Oxford Press, 1968.

Duncan, Hugh Dalziel, *Symbols in Society*, London: Oxford Press, 1968.

Grinker, Roy R., ed., *Toward a Unified Theory of Human Behavior: An Introduction to General Systems Theory*, New York: Basic Books, 1956, 1967.

Johnson, Wendell, *People in Quandaries*, New York: Harper & Row, 1946.

MacLean, Malcolm S., Jr., "A Process Concept of Communication Education: A Position Statement for the Educational Policies Committee." School of Journalism, University of Iowa, 1966 (mimeo).

MacLean, Malcolm S., Jr., "Theory, Method and Games in Communication." Paper prepared for a meeting of the behavioral science section of the International Association for Mass Communication Research, Ljubljana, Yugoslavia, September, 1968.

MacLean, Malcolm S., Jr., and Albert D. Talbott, "Approaches to Speech-Communication Theory Through Simulation and Games." Paper presented at the Speech Association of America/International Communication Association Annual Meeting, New York City, December, 1969.

Nylen, Donald, J. Robert Mitchell and Anthony Stout, *Handbook of Staff Development and Human Relations Training: Materials Developed for Use in Africa,* Washington: National Training Laboratories, Institute for Applied Behavioral Science, 1967.

Postman, Neil and Charles Weingartner, *Teaching as a Subversive Activity,* New York: Delacorte Press, 1969.

Ruben, Brent D. and John Y. Kim, *Human Communication and General Systems Theory,* Rochelle Park, N.J.: Hayden (in press).

Ruben, Brent D. "The What and Why of Gaming, A Taxonomy of Experiential Learning Systems," in *Proceedings 1973,* National Gaming Council, Gaithersburg, Maryland.

Ruesch, Jurgen and Gregory Bateson, *Communication: The Social Matrix of Psychiatry,* New York: W. W. Norton, 1968, 1951.

Schroder, Harold M., Michael J. Driver and Siegfried Streufert, *Human Information Processing,* New York: Holt, Rinehart and Winston, 1967.

Thayer, Lee, *Communication and Communication Systems,* Homewood, Ill.: Richard D. Irwin, 1968.

Thayer, Lee, "Communication—Sine Qua Non of the Behavioral Sciences," in *Vistas in Science,* D. L. Arm, ed., University of New Mexico Press, 1968.

Upton, Albert, *Design for Thinking,* Stanford: Stanford University Press, 1961.

Vickers, Sir Geoffrey, *Value Systems and Social Process,* New York: Basic Books, 1968.

Young, J. Z., *Doubt and Certainty in Science: A Biologist's Reflections on the Brain,* New York: Galaxy Books, Oxford University Press, 1960.

Experience-Based Learning Theory

Archambault, Reginald, *Lectures in the Philosophy of Education: 1899 by John Dewey,* New York: Random House, 1966.

Bruner, J. S., *Learning About Learning: A Conference Report,* Washington: U.S. Government Printing Office, 1966.

Bruner, J. S., *The Process of Education,* Cambridge, Mass.: Harvard Press, 1961.

Bruner, J. S., *The Relevance of Education*, New York: Norton, 1971.

Bruner, J. S., *Toward a Theory of Instruction,* New York: Norton, 1966.

Bruner, J. S., Rose R. Oliver and Patricia M. Greenfield, *et. al., Studies in Cognitive Growth,* New York: Wiley, 1966.

Budd, Richard W., "Communication, Education and Simulation: Some Thought on the Learning Process," Institute for Communication Studies, University of Iowa, Iowa City, Iowa, December, 1970.

Budd, Richard W., "The Impact of the Mass Media on Curricula," in Richard W. Burns and Gary D. Brooks, eds., *Curriculum Design in a Changing Society,* Englewood Cliffs, N.J.: Educational Technology Press, 1972.

Danish, Paul, *Champaign Report: A Conference on Educational Reform —A Student View,* Champaign, Ill., September, 1966.

Dewey, John, *Experience and Education*, New York: Macmillan, 1938.

Gardner, John W., *Self-Renewal: The Individual and the Innovative Society,* New York: Harper & Row, 1965.

Harvey, O. J., *Experience, Structure and Adaptability,* New York: Springer, 1966.

MacLean, Malcolm S., Jr., "A Process Concept of Communication Education: A Position Statement for the Educational Policies Committee," School of Journalism, University of Iowa, 1966.

Montessori, Maria, *Spontaneous Activity in Education,* New York: Schocken, 1965.

Neill, A. S., *Summerhill: A Radical Approach to Child Rearing,* New York: Hart, 1960.

Postman, Neil and Charles Weingartner, *Teaching as a Subversive Activity*, New York: Delacorte, 1969.

Riesman, David, *Constraint and Variety of American Education,* Lincoln, Nebr.: University of Nebraska Press, 1968.

Rogers, Carl R., *Freedom to Learn,* Columbus, Ohio: Charles E. Merrill, 1969.

Ruben, Brent D., *Interact,* Kennebunkport, Maine: Mercer House Press, 1973.

Ruben, Brent D., "The What and Why of Gaming: A Taxonomy of Experiential Learning Systems," in *Proceedings 1973* of the Annual Symposium of The National Gaming Council and the International Simulation and Gaming Association, Gaithersburg, Maryland, 1973.

Ruben, Brent D. and Albert D. Talbott, "Communication, Information and Education Systems: Some Perspectives," paper presented to the 17th Annual Conference of the National Society for the Study of Communication, Cleveland, Ohio, 1969.

Schroder, Harold M., Michael J. Driver and Siegfried Streufert, *Human Information Processing,* New York: Holt, Rinehart & Winston, 1967.

Shulman, Lee S. and Evan R. Keisler, ed., *Learning by Discovery: A Critical Appraisal,* Chicago: Rand McNally, 1966.

Thayer, Lee, "On Communication and Change: Some Provocations," *Systematics,* Vol. 6, No. 3, December, 1968.

Upton, Albert, *Design for Thinking,* Stanford: Stanford University Press, 1961.

Instructional Simulations and Games

Abt, Clark C., *Serious Games,* New York: Viking, 1970.

Armstrong, R. H. R. and R. J. Taylor, *Instructional Simulation Systems in Higher Education,* Cambridge, Mass.: Cambridge University Press, 1970.

Attig, J. C., "Use of Games as a Teaching Technique," in *Social Studies,* Vol. 58, January, 1967.

Boocock, Sarane S., "Games Change What Goes on in the Classroom," in *Nation's Schools,* Vol. 80, October, 1967.

Boocock, Sarane S., "Instructional Games," in *Encyclopedia of Education,* New York: Macmillan, 1971.

Boocock, Sarane S. and James S. Coleman, "Games with Simulated Environments in Learning," in *Sociology of Education,* Vol. 39, Summer, 1966.

Boocock, Sarane S. and E. O. Schild, eds., *Simulation Games in Learning,* Beverly Hills, Calif.: Sage, 1971.

Burgess, Philip, "Organizing Simulated Environments," in *Social Education,* Vol. 33, February, 1969.

Carlson, Elliot, *Learning through Games,* Washington, D.C.: Public Affairs Press, 1969.

Cherryholmes, Cleo H., "Some Current Research on Effectiveness of Educational Simulations: Implications for Alternative Strategies," in *American Behavioral Scientist,* Vol. X, No. 2, October, 1966.

Cohen, Kalman J. and Eric Rhenman, "The Role of Management Games in Education and Research," in *Management Science,* Vol. 7, 1961.

Coleman, James S., "Games as Vehicles for Social Theory," in *American Behavioral Scientist,* Vol. 12, July-August, 1969.

Coleman, James S., "Learning Through Games," in *NEA Journal,* Vol. 56, January, 1967.

Coleman, James S., "Simulation Games and Social Theory," Baltimore, Md.: Center for the Study of Social Organization of Schools, Johns Hopkins University, Report No. 8, 1968. (mimeo)

Crawford, Meredith P., "Dimensions of Simulation," in *American Psychologist,* Vol. 21, No. 8, August, 1966.

Dill, William R. and Neil Doppelt, "The Acquisition of Experience in a Complex Management Game," in *Management Science,* Vol. 10, No. 1, October, 1963.

Fennessey, Gail M., Samuel A. Livingston, Keith J. Edwards, Steven J. Kidder, and Alyce W. Nafziger, "Simulation, Gaming and Conventional Instruction: An Experimental Comparison," Baltimore, Md.: Center for Social Organization of Schools, Johns Hopkins University, Report No. 128, 1972.

Fletcher, Jerry L., "The Effectiveness of Simulation Games as Learning Environments: A Proposed Program of Research," in *Simulation and Games,* Vol. 2, December, 1971.

Fletcher, Jerry L., "Evaluation of Learning in Two Social Studies Simulation Games," in *Simulation and Games,* Vol. 2, September, 1971.

Gamson, William A., "SIMSOC: Establishing Social Order in a Simulated Society," in *Simulation and Games,* Vol. 2, September, 1971.

Gordon, Alice Kaplan, *Games for Growth,* Palo Alto, Calif.: Science Research Associates, 1970.

Greenblat, Cathy S., "Gaming and Simulation in the Social Sciences," in *A Guide to the Literature,* New Brunswick, N.J.: Douglass College, Rutgers University, 1972.

Greenblatt, Cathy S., Simulations, Games and the Sociologist," in *The American Sociologist,* Vol. 6, May, 1971.

Greenblat, Cathy S., "Teaching with Simulation Games: A Review of Claims and Evidence," in *Teaching Sociology,* Vol. 1, October, 1972.

Hearn, Edell M. and Thomas Reddick, *Simulated Behavioral Teaching Situations,* Dubuque, Iowa: W. C. Brown, 1971.

Inbar, Michael, "Participating in a Simulation Game," in *The Journal of Applied Behavioral Science,* Vol. 6, 1970.

Inbar, Michael and C. S. Stoll, eds., *Simulation and Gaming in Social Science,* New York: Free Press, 1972.

Kasperson, Roger E., "Games as Educational Media," in *Journal of Geography,* Vol. 62, October, 1968.

Kidder, Steven J., *Simulation Games: Practical References, Potential Use, Selected Bibliography,* Baltimore, Md.: Center for Social Organization of Schools, Johns Hopkins University, 1971.

Klietsch, Ronald, *An Introduction to Learning Games and Instructional Simulations,* St. Paul, Minn.: Instructional Simulations, 1969.

Klietsch, Ronald and Fred Wiegman, *Directory of Educational Simulations, Learning Games, and Didactic Units,* St. Paul, Minn.: Instructional Simulations, 1969.

MacLean, Malcolm S., Jr., "Theory, Method and Games in Communication," in *Mass Media and International Understanding,* France Vreg, ed., Ljubljana, Yugoslavia: School of Sociology, Political Science and Journalism, Part I, 1969.

MacLean, Malcolm S., Jr. and Albert D. Talbott, "Approaches to Speech-Communication Theory Through Simulation and Games," paper presented at the Speech Association of American/International Communication Association Annual Meeting, New York City, December, 1969.

McKenney, James and William R. Dill, "Influences on Learning in

Simulation Games," in *American Behavioral Scientist,* Vol. 10, October, 1966.

Pitts, Forrest, *The Varieties of Simulation: A Review and Bibliography,* Philadelphia: Regional Science Research Institute.

Raser, John R., *Simulation and Society: An Exploration of Scientific Gaming,* Boston: Allyn and Bacon, 1969.

Raser, John R., Donald T. Campbell and Richard W. Chadwick, "Gaming and Simulation for Developing Theory Relevant to International Relations," in *General Systems,* Ludwig von Bertalanffy and Anatol Rapoport, eds., Washington, D.C.: Society for General Systems Research, 1970.

Robinson, James, "Simulation and Games," in *The New Media and Education,* Peter Rossi and Bruce Biddle, eds., Chicago: Aldine, 1966.

Ruben, Brent D., *Interact,* Kennebunkport, Maine: Mercer House Press, 1973.

Ruben, Brent D., "The What and Why of Gaming: A Taxonomy of Experiential Learning Systems," in *Proceedings 1973* of the Annual Symposium of The National Gaming Council and the International Simulation and Gaming Association, Gaithersburg, Maryland, 1973.

Ruben, Brent D. and Albert D. Talbott, "The Communication System Simulation: An Overview," Iowa City, Iowa: University of Iowa, January, 1970. (mimeo)

Ruben, Brent D., Albert D. Talbott, Lee M. Brown and Henry G. LaBrie, *Intermedia: Participant's Manual,* Iowa City, Iowa: University Associates Press, 1970.

"Selective Bibliography on Simulation Games as Learning Devices," in *American Behavioral Scientist,* Vol. 10, November, 1966.

Talbott, Albert D. and Brent D. Ruben, *Communication System Simulation Participant's Manual,* Iowa City, Iowa: University of Iowa, School of Journalism, 1970. (mimeo)

Tansey, P. J., ed., *Education Aspects of Simulation,* Maidenhead, England: McGraw-Hill, 1971.

Tansey, P. J. "Simulation Techniques in the Training of Teachers," in *Simulation and Games,* Vol. 1, September, 1970.

Thayer, Lee, *Studies in the Development of Administrators: II An Experimental Training Program,* Wichita, Kansas: College of Business Administration, Wichita State University, 1964.

Twelker, Paul A., ed., *Instructional Simulation Systems,* Corvallis, Oregon: Continuing Education Publications, Oregon State University, Department of Printing, 1969.

Werner, Roland and Joan T. Werner, *Bibliography of Simulations: Social Systems and Education,* LaJolla, Calif.: Western Behavioral Sciences Institute, 1969.

Wilson, J. P. and D. E. Adams, "A Selected Bibliography of Simulations and Related Subject, 1960–1969," Pittsburg, Kansas: Political Science, Kansas State College, April 6, 1970.

Youngers, John C. and John F. Aceti, *Simulation Games and Activities for Social Studies,* Dansville, N.Y.: The Instructor Publications, 1969.

Zieler, Richard, *Games for School Use: An Annotated List,* Yorktown Heights, N.Y.: Board of Cooperative Educational Services.

Zuckerman, David W. and Robert E. Horn, *The Guide to Simulation Games for Education and Training,* Cambridge, Mass.: Information Resources, 1970.

Instructional Role Playing and Structured Exercises

Bavelas, Alex, "Role Playing and Management Training," *Sociatry,* Vol. 1, No. 2, June, 1947.

Blansfield, Michael G., "Role-Playing as a Method in Executive Development," *Personnel Journal,* Vol. 34, 1953.

Chesler, Mark and Robert Fox, *Role-Playing Methods in the Classroom,* Chicago: Science Research Associates, 1966.

Corsini, Raymond J., Malcolm E. Shaw and Robert R. Blake, *Roleplaying, in Business and Industry,* New York: Free Press, 1961.

Elms, Alan C., *Role Playing, Reward and Attitude Change,* New York: Van Nostrand-Reinhold, 1971.

Lowell, Mildred H., *Role Playing and Other Management Cases,* Metuchen, N.J.: Scarecrow, 1971.

Mann, John H., "Experimental Evaluations of Role Playing," *Psychological Bulletin,* Vol. 53, No. 3, May, 1956.

Mial, Dorothy J. and Stanley Jacobson, "10 Interaction Exercises for the Classroom," Washington: National Training Laboratory, Institute for Applied Behavioral Science.

Moreno, J. L., *Psychodrama,* Vol. 1, New York: Beacon, 1946.

Nylen, Donald J., Robert Mitchell and Anthony Stout, *Handbook of Staff Development and Human Relations Training: Materials Developed for Use in Africa,* Washington: National Training Laboratory, Institute for Applied Behavioral Science, 1967.

Parnes, Sidney J., *Creative Behavior Guidebook,* New York: Scribner's, 1967.

Parnes, Sidney J., *Creative Behavior Workbook,* New York: Scribner's, 1967.

Pfeiffer, J. William and John E. Jones, *A Handbook of Structured Experiences for Human Relations Training, Volume I,* La Jolla, Calif.: University Associates, 1969.

Pfeiffer, J. William and John E. Jones, *A Handbook of Structured Experiences for Human Relations Training, Volume II,* La Jolla, Calif.: University Associates, 1970.

Pfeiffer, J. William and John E. Jones, *A Handbook of Structured Experiences for Human Relations Training, Volume III*, La Jolla, Calif.: University Associates, 1971.

Pfeiffer, J. William and John E. Jones, *The 1972 Annual Handbook for Group Facilitators*, La Jolla, Calif.: University Associates Press, 1972.

Scher, Jordan M., "Two Disruptions of the Communication Zone: A Discussion of Action and Role Playing Techniques," *Group Psychotherapy*, Vol. XII, No. 2, June, 1959.

Shaftel, Fannie R., *Role-Playing for Social Values: Decision-Making in the Social Studies*, Englewood Cliffs, N.J.: Prentice-Hall, 1967.

Part 1
PERSONAL COMMUNICATION

Serving sometimes as a communicator, initiator, or mass communicator of information; sometimes as a recipient, receiver or audience member; and often more or less simultaneously as both, the *individual* is clearly at the center of the communication process. To understand how the personal communication process operates, it is useful to consider how we function as users and creators of verbal, written, and non-verbal messages. More specifically, one might focus upon how we see, hear, gather, order, categorize, and understand the situations in which we find ourselves. This handbook emphasizes the role of assumptions, past experience, language, perception, and expectations in influencing our notion of self, objects, environment, and other people, as well as our own values and our ability to learn and to change at any point in time. In adopting such a view of personal communication, we are concerned as much about how we are communicated-with as we are about how we communicate-to.

Upon first consideration, it might seem that most people are communicated-with, and to some extent also communicate-to, in more or less the same way. It often seems, for example, that when we talk with others about experiences that all were present for, such as a course lecture, that there is a general agreement as to what the experience was about—in this case the lecture. And it is true that in many circumstances there seems to be enough common perceptions and interpretations between individuals, to safely assume that other people will behave toward a particular word, picture, or event more or less as we do.

But this is an assumption that fails at least as often as it works, and is particularly dangerous if one is unaware of the concept of personal communication. It is seldom indeed that the interpretations of two individuals overlap and correspond enough to treat them as one and the same. To note that we buy different cars, perfumes, toothpastes; prefer different colors, read different magazines, newspapers, and television programs; live in different sorts of dwellings; belong to different clubs, political parties, and professional organizations; and have different friends, is to point out only the tip of the iceberg of individual difference. And it is largely through the processes of personal communication that we acquire, maintain, and alter our manner of making choices, relating and sorting information about our world and the people in it. And clearly, differences in our choices are reflective of more basic differences in the way in which we perceive, experience, observe, categorize, interpret, and value aspects of our environment.

It is not difficult to intellectually document the fact that there are differences from person to person in the way they view people and things in their environment, and in terms of the sorts of assumptions and expectations they apply. The problem is that while the idea isn't difficult to grasp *in theory,* it is extremely difficult to apply to one's own behavior *in practice.* How often we find ourselves shocked and surprised when a friend or acquaintance assumes that we meant one thing, when we *knew* we meant something quite different. Too often we find ourselves behaving as if our understandings or interpretations were *the* understandings, which were *right* or *true.* And, of course, to the extent that we are victimized by this orientation we are closed off from the very information and people who might stimulate us to reexamine and change this attitude.

Of additional importance is the evaluation of our effectiveness as communicators, which can be measured only by taking into account the intended audience and their responses to our intentions. And to the extent that one is unaware of or unconcerned with the responses of other people around him to his communicative efforts, he will be successful as a communicator only on a random basis. It is probably a realization of this complex situation which led to the authoring of the increasingly popular phrase, "I know you believe you understand what you think I said, but I am not sure you realize that what you heard is not what I meant."

The activities in this section of the book deal directly with aspects of the personal communication process, focusing both on communicating-to and being communicated-with, in written, verbal and non-verbal modes. In general the intent is to heighten participant awareness of how personal communication operates and the role each individual plays intentionally, or not, in its outcome. Accordingly, exercises are included which deal with listening, self-disclosure, self-perception, values, interpersonal perception, closure, experience and language, environmental awareness, categorization, context, perceptual patterns, learning and change, assumptions, observation, inference, attitudes, silence, personal space, paralanguage, eye contact patterns, situational geography, and kinesics. Each activity is intended to raise questions, to stimulate discussion, and to foster introspection. There is no single correct interpretation of any of the games or simulations presented, nor are there any necessarily right or wrong ways of using them. We suggest one set of procedures for each concept presented, and encourage users to modify and adapt them to their particular instructional needs. There is no attempt to provide a single statement of encompassing theory to accompany any activity presented, but only to provide a basic skeletal framework. The accompanying selective bibliography is highly recommended for readers who wish to maximize their skills in utilizing these activities.

1. Self-Disclosure and Listening

This activity is designed to focus attention on the basic aspects of speaking, listening, and self-disclosure. The activity requires approximately 30 minutes and can be used with any number of three-person groups.

Procedure:

1. Participants are clustered in triads.
2. Members of each triad assign themselves the letter A, B, or C. The triad member designated A will serve initially in the role of *speaker*. Person B in each triad will serve first as *listener,* and person C will act in the role of *judge*.
3. The task of the individual designated A in each triad, is to briefly present (3 to 5 minutes) to persons B and C, a description of those things about him which another person would need to know in order to understand how and why he communicates as he does.
4. At the conclusion of the 3–5 minute period, person A concludes his presentation. Person B, who has been serving as listener, then provides a verbal summary of the main points of person A's explanation.
5. The summary must satisfy person C who judges the accuracy and adequacy of person B's listening and summarization.
6. After having satisfied persons A and C, person B moves into the role of speaker, and explains to persons A (who now serves as judge) and C (who serves as listener) what they would need to know about him in order to understand how and why he communicates as he does.
7. After 3–5 minutes person C summarizes what person B has said and then, after satisfying persons B and A, becomes the speaker.
8. The process may be repeated several times allowing each participant the opportunity to serve more than once in each role.

Discussion:

In general, discussion centers on the nature of the roles of speaker, listener, and judge, the relations between them, and the problems associated with serving in each position. Participants may wish to discuss whether the structure and rules of the game facilitated or hindered the communication process. It will also be interesting to note the difficulty participants encounter in listening to what others are saying, as opposed to thinking about how they themselves are reacting to the other persons, the situation, and their own responses to the subject at hand. What difficulties did participants experience in the role of speaker? listener? judge? What was done or could have been done to alleviate these difficulties? Did the personal nature of the subject matter under discussion facilitate or inhibit? Which aspects of the game and its outcomes can be usefully generalized to everyday communication situations?

2. Self Perception and Value Orientation

This exercise is designed to foster an increased awareness of an individual's self perception and value hierarchy, and to sharpen skills in self description. The activity requires approximately 30 minutes and can be used in groups ranging from several to 50 participants.

Procedure:

1. Each participant is asked to list on a sheet of paper the five most important things about him or herself, from his own point of view. Allow 3–8 minutes for this portion of the exercise.
2. After participants have completed their lists, they are asked to pair off.
3. Instructions are given for each member of a dyad, in turn, to read his list of five personal characteristics to his partner, and to discuss similarities and differences. Allow 5–10 minutes for this phase.
4. Each dyad is asked to join with two other dyads, forming a six-person group.
5. Each of the six participants introduces his dyad partner to the other four group members, describing him in terms of the five characteristics the individual himself listed. The introduction may also draw on information acquired during the discussion of differences and similarities.
6. Following the introduction of each of the six participants by their dyad partner, the group discusses differences and similarities between lists and their reaction to the activity as a whole.

Discussion:

The instructor may wish the entire group of participants to discuss the general implications of this exercise, in addition to the more specific discussions which take place within the dyadic and six-person groups. These conversations may focus upon the extent to which the five items participants list, reflect more generalized value orientations. In this connection it may be useful to explore how different individuals decide what characteristics about themselves to list. Would the items selected for listing have been different if the individuals had known one another better? In addition to self-perception, discussion can explore whether or not participants were conscious of listing items which would project a particular image to others. Where such is the case, comparisons can be made between the intended image and the actual image received by others. What were the reactions to the idea of disclosing five characteristics to another person? How much were dyad members able to learn about their partners from the items listed? From the discussion which followed? What were the reactions to being introduced by the dyad partner to a new group of people? Which aspects of this exercise and its outcomes have applicability in everyday communication situations? This activity also provides the basis for discussing skills and problems associated with listening.

3. Seeing and Not Seeing

These demonstrations typically referred to as "perceptual illusions," illustrate how initial viewing of an object or person may lead to incorrect or incomplete conclusions. Additionally, the activity suggests by implication, that it is difficult to impossible to view one thing in two ways at the same time. The activity requires fifteen minutes to one half hour and can be used with any number of participants.

Procedure:
1. Reproduce any of the illustrations provided in Figs. 3.1–3.5 on a screen or present to a group by holding up the visual itself.
2. Ask participants in each case what the picture depicts.

Discussion:
After some time participants will notice that Fig. 3.1 can be viewed as either an old woman (facing the right side of the photo) or a young and attractive lady (whose right cheek is visible). Fig. 3.2 is seen both as a vase and two people facing one another. Fig. 3.3, depending upon

Fig. 3.1

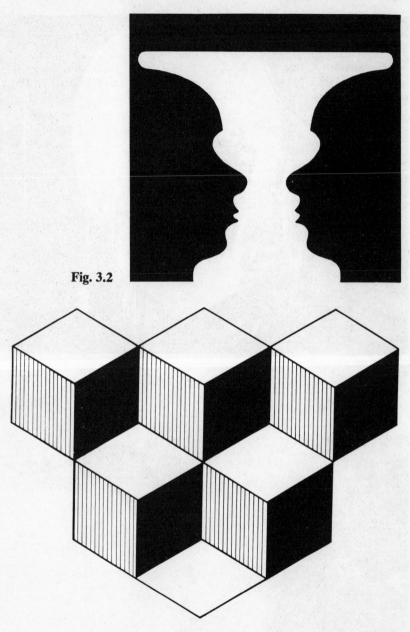

Fig. 3.2

Fig. 3.3

one's perspective, appears as either three or five blocks. Fig. 3.4 appears first as a skull and subsequently participants will note a lady viewing herself in a mirror. Fig. 3.5 appears as many different things to participants and eventually some will decide that it is a cow. (See outline on Fig. 3.6).

Fig. 3.4

Fig. 3.5

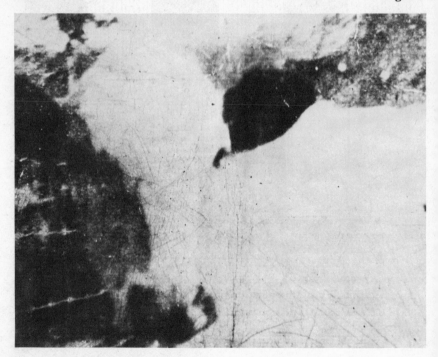

Fig. 3.6

4. Closure

This demonstration is intended to illustrate the significance of past experiences and expectations as determinants of present perceptions and conceptions. The activity requires five to ten minutes and can be used with any number of participants.

Procedure:

1. Reproduce either of the illustrations provided in Figs. 4.1 or 4.2 on a flip chart, blackboard, or screen.
2. Ask participants what the picture portrays.

Discussion:

How certain were participants of what they think they saw? After reshowing the illustrations, discuss the impact of past experience on the perception of current events. If not brought out by participants, it will be useful to simply note that we tend to see a dog rather than merely

Fig. 4.1

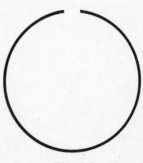

Fig. 4.2

a collection of ink blots, because we fill in the form as we perceive it based upon our previous experience with objects which seem similar. The same pattern is of course true with the other illustration, where even though merely an arc, we tend to perceive the figure as a circle. How did expectations in combination with being *asked* what participants saw, affect perceptions? What relevance does this kind of process have for everyday perception and communication?

5. Experience and Language

This demonstration illustrates the influence of past experience and expectation upon perception, and is usefully presented as a part of a discussion of those concepts. The demonstration requires approximately 10 minutes and can be used with any size group.

Procedure:

1. One of the signs provided in Figs. 5.1 and 5.2 is held up in front of the participant group for several seconds.
2. The sign is removed from their view and they are asked to indicate out loud what the sign said.
3. The sign again is presented to the group for several seconds, after which they are asked to indicate what they saw.
4. The cycle is repeated until a number of the participants become aware of their mistakes or until such time as the instructor wishes to begin discussion of the concepts.

Discussion:

Experience with language, and in this case experience with sentences, is one important force in shaping the nature of our reactions to our environment and the meanings we perceive, as this exercise clearly demonstrates. For purposes of discussion one might involve participants

Fig. 5.1

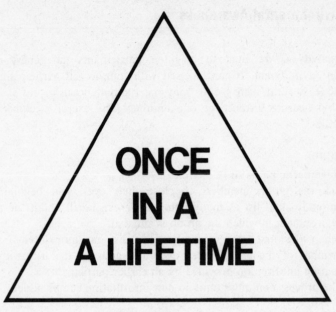

Fig. 5.2

by asking, "What happened?" at the conclusion of the exercise. Why did participants perceive incorrectly? What are some of the implications of this exercise for understanding the nature of human communication?

6. Environmental Awareness

This activity is designed to heighten participants' awareness of their physical environment. It can be used with four to ten participants seated in a circle. Several such groups may meet simultaneously, but should not be within hearing distance of one another. The exercise requires 10 to 15 minutes.

Procedure:

1. Have participants sit in a circle.
2. Ask the group members to close their eyes, and beginning with one individual list as many items as he can recall about the physical environment in which the group is situated.
3. When the first group member can list no more items, another member of the group takes over and adds to the list, without repeating information provided by an earlier participant.
4. The process continues until no new information can be added.

Discussion:

Each of us experiences sensory stimuli in different ways. Some individuals are particularly conscious of colors, some of smells, others of spatial relationships. Some remember minute details, others take in overall tones and textures or moods. How observant were participants? What kinds of things were particularly well remembered? Were there different patterns of perception and recall for different individuals? What aspects of an environment were particularly important to *you?* What elements tend to get ignored?

7. Categorization

This exercise is intended to be used to initiate discussions of the process of classification, and the influence of experience and language in pattern perception. The activity requires approximately 10 minutes and can be used with any size group.

Procedure:
1. Reproduce Figs. 7.1, 7.2 or 7.3 on a flip chart, blackboard, or handout.
2. Participants are then asked to describe and discuss the drawings.

Discussion:
In describing Fig. 7.1, most participants will see and describe the image in terms of broken squares or pairs of brackets as opposed to other classifications and descriptions. One such alternative would be a pattern with clustered units by dividing the open area between the "brackets". The result would be "I" shaped images with enlarged centers.

Descriptions of Fig. 7.2 will tend to categorize and describe the pattern in terms of pairs of two, close parallel lines, as opposed to alternative characterizations in terms, for example, of the parallel lines which are further from one another.

In Fig. 7.3, participants typically offer the description in terms of lines of circles and lines of dots, as opposed for example to lines composed alternately of circles and dots.

The way individuals categorize and describe the relationships in their environment, depends not only upon physiological constraints, but upon past experience and language patterns as well. This demonstration can serve as the initial input for a discussion of the relationship between established language components and patterns (e.g. "square") and the ways in which we categorize and describe what we see around us. How

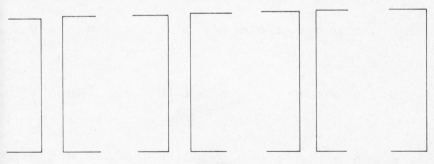

Fig. 7.1

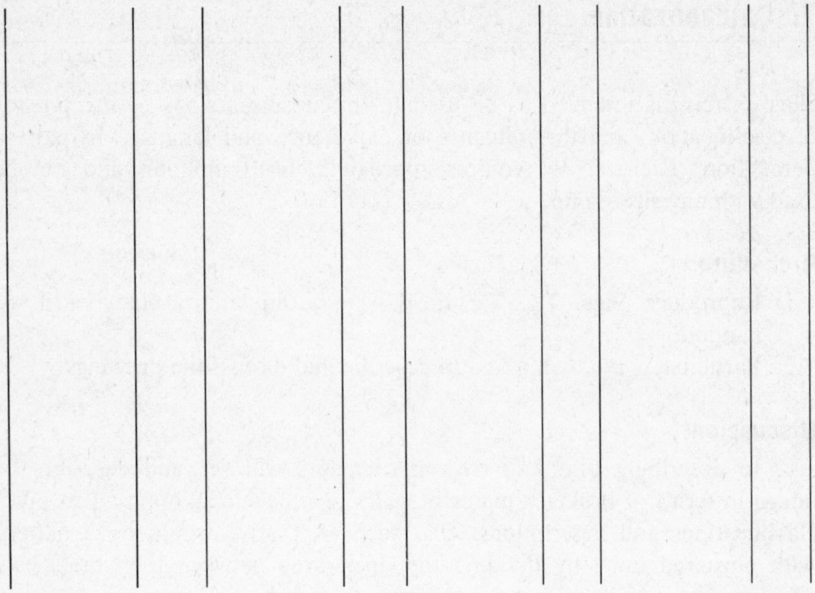

Fig. 7.2

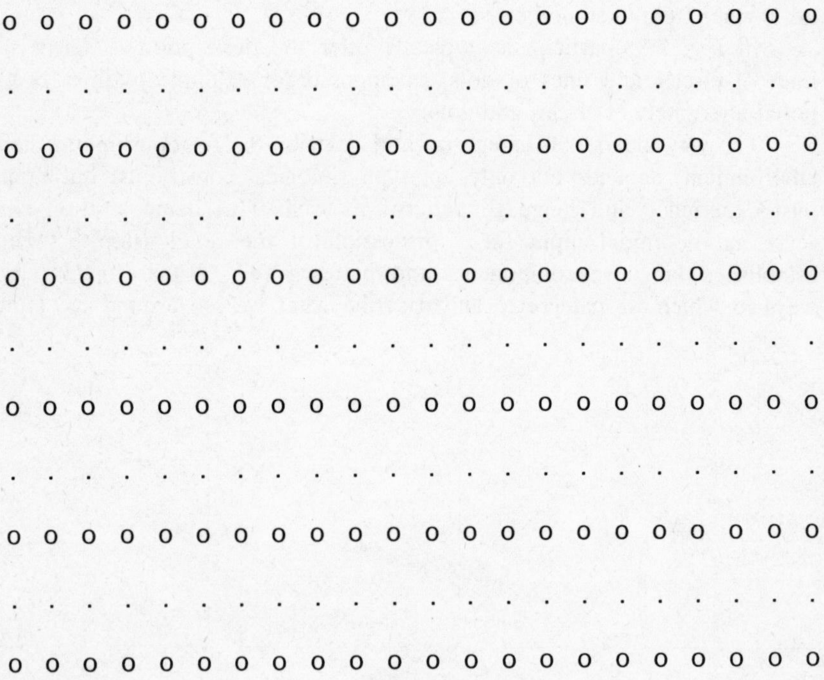

Fig. 7.3

does this relationship influence the way we perceive situations in normal everyday contexts? In what ways do past experience and language patterns influence the way we categorize people? Can categorization be a barrier to creativity?

8. Perceptual Context

This exercise involves the use of drawings which foster perceptual illusions; each is useful not only for stimulating discussions of how easily perceptions can be inaccurate, but additionally for noting the importance of context, or surroundings, as a factor in determining what we perceive.

Procedure:

1. Reproduce Figs. 8.1, 8.2, 8.3, 8.4, 8.5, or any combination thereof on a flip chart, blackboard, or screen.
2. Participants are then asked to describe the images. Particular focus is directed toward having participants decide which line is longer? (Fig. 8.1 and 8.2); are the lines parallel? (Fig. 8.3); are line segment "a" and line segment "b" part of a straight line? (Fig. 8.4); is the non-triangle figure a circle? (Fig. 8.5)

Discussion:

In each illustration the context in which the focal objects are placed, contributes to misperceptions. In Figs. 8.1 and 8.2, line "a" appears longer than line "b", but they are equal in length. In Fig. 8.3 the long lines appear not to be parallel to one another, but are. In Fig. 8.4 line segments "a" and "b" are part of a straight line. In Fig. 8.5 the non-triangular figure is a circle. What factors contributed to the way these illustrations were perceived? If the exercise was conducted in a

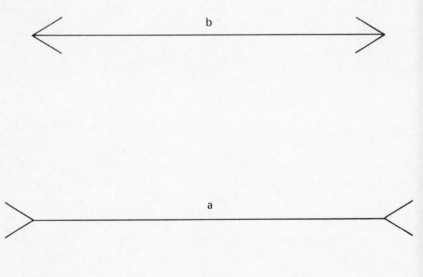

Fig. 8.1

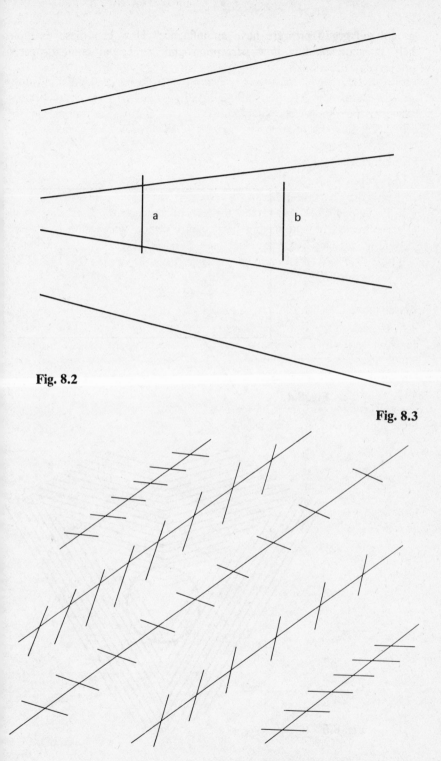

Fig. 8.2

Fig. 8.3

group, did group pressure have an influence? How can these examples help in understanding how perception and perceptual context operate in everyday situations?

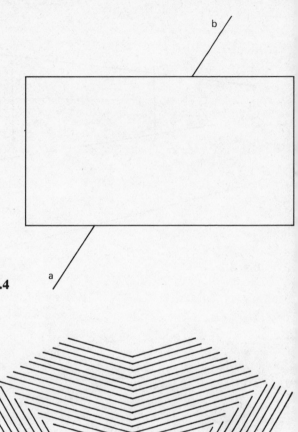

Fig. 8.4

Fig. 8.5

9. Object Awareness

This exercise is designed to raise questions about assumptions, past experience, and their influence on problem-solving. The activity can be used with any number of participants and requires approximately 10 minutes.

Procedure:
1. The letters *IX* are put on a screen, flip chart, or blackboard as shown in Fig. 9.1.
2. Participants are told that the problem to be solved is to make six out of IX by making a single change.

Discussion:

Rarely do participants come up with the obvious correct solution —adding an *S* at the beginning of the *IX* as shown in Fig. 9.2. Generally, they assume that the solution has to do with roman numerals, or approach the lines as something other than letters. There are other solutions as shown in Fig. 9.2. Others may be discovered that reflect different approaches to the problem.

What factors act as barriers to solving the exercise? In what ways could creativity have been utilized in solving the problem? In what ways is this problem similar to problems in other everyday communication situations?

IX Fig. 9.1

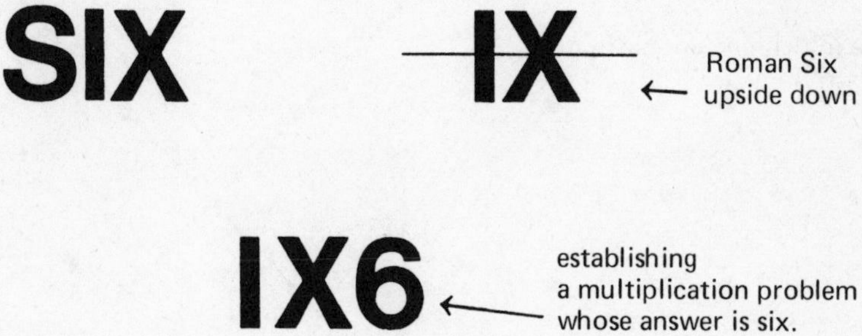

SIX   **IX** Roman Six ← upside down

IX6 ← establishing a multiplication problem whose answer is six.

Fig. 9.2

10. Perceptual Set

This puzzle is designed to stimulate discussion about perceptual set and its influence on problem solving. The activity requires about 10 minutes and can be used with groups of any size.

Procedure:

1. Nine dots are placed on a flip chart or blackboard in the pattern shown in Fig. 10.1.
2. Participants are told that their task is to connect all nine dots with *four straight lines*. The rules are: a) You can cross another line. b) You cannot retrace a line. c) You cannot lift the pencil or pen from beginning the first line until ending the fourth.
3. After several minutes of working on the problem, ask if any of the participants have a solution. You might then ask them to show the other participants their solution and explain how they arrived at it.

Discussion:

In the particular problem posed by this exercise, the difficulty in arriving at a solution comes about because participants tend to see the dots as a square. See solution provided in Fig. 10.2. They further assume that their four lines may not go outside of the assumed boundary provided by that square. Why is the problem difficult to solve? What applicability does this puzzle have for everyday communication encounters?

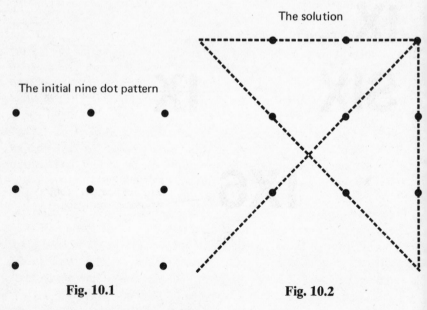

The solution

The initial nine dot pattern

Fig. 10.1   **Fig. 10.2**

11. Learning and Change

The exercise centers on the processes of gathering, categorizing, and modifying information patterns. The exercise can be used with a group of any size: it requires approximately 20 minutes. The exercise is appropriately used in conjunction with other activities focusing on communication and change.

Procedure:

1. The Instructor should make up and distribute a set of numbered sheets to each participant, reproducing Fig. 11.1 (which will be sheets 1 through 4) and Fig. 11.2. (which will be sheet No. 5.) A covering sheet (preferably colored) will carry the following instructions:

    PLEASE DO NOT OPEN UNTIL TOLD TO DO SO.

    COUNT TO BE SURE THAT YOU HAVE FIVE SHEETS IN ADDITION TO THIS COLORED SHEET. *DO NOT LOOK AT THE OTHER SHEETS.*

    LISTEN CAREFULLY FOR FURTHER INSTRUCTIONS BEFORE DOING ANYTHING ELSE. (Prior to distributing the booklets, the instructor should check each one carefully to insure that the first four pages are the same (use Fig. 11.1) and that the final page is different from the others (use Fig. 11.2.).

2. Cautioning the participants not to open their booklets, explain the following:

    This exercise is very much like doing a children's dot-to-dot puzzle. When you open your booklets, you will easily locate the number *1* in the upper left-hand corner because it has been circled for you. Your task is to then locate the number *2,* and with a pencil draw a line from *1* to *2;* then locate the number *3* and draw a line from *2* to *3,* and so forth. Continue on in this manner, working as rapidly as you can until I say "stop." When I tell you to stop, draw a circle around the last number you have been able to locate, and wait for further instructions. *Do not turn to the second page until I tell you to do so.*

    (You may find it useful during the description to give a brief blackboard demonstration by randomly locating several numbers on the board and drawing appropriate lines from one to the other.)

3. When it is clear all participants understand the procedures, tell them to turn to page one and begin. Keeping careful track of the time, allow work to continue for *45 seconds.* When time has elapsed, insist that everyone stop and circle the last number located.

1 33 9 25 23 45
49 45 37 59 13
35 15 21 29
19 51 1 55
3 27 47
11 31
43 57 17 53 39
5
34 12 36 20 56 22
46
2 54
18 40 8
28 58 14
50 30
38 48
42 26 44 6
24
4 10 52 32 60 16

Fig. 11.1

4. Before beginning page two, tell participants that they will now re-do the exercise, but this time they will have the experience gained in the first run through to assist them. Again, tell participants to begin, again allowing only 45 seconds of work time.

5. Before beginning page three, ask participants to take their booklets —using the page they have just completed—and fold them (without creasing them) in half *horizontally* and to compare the top of the

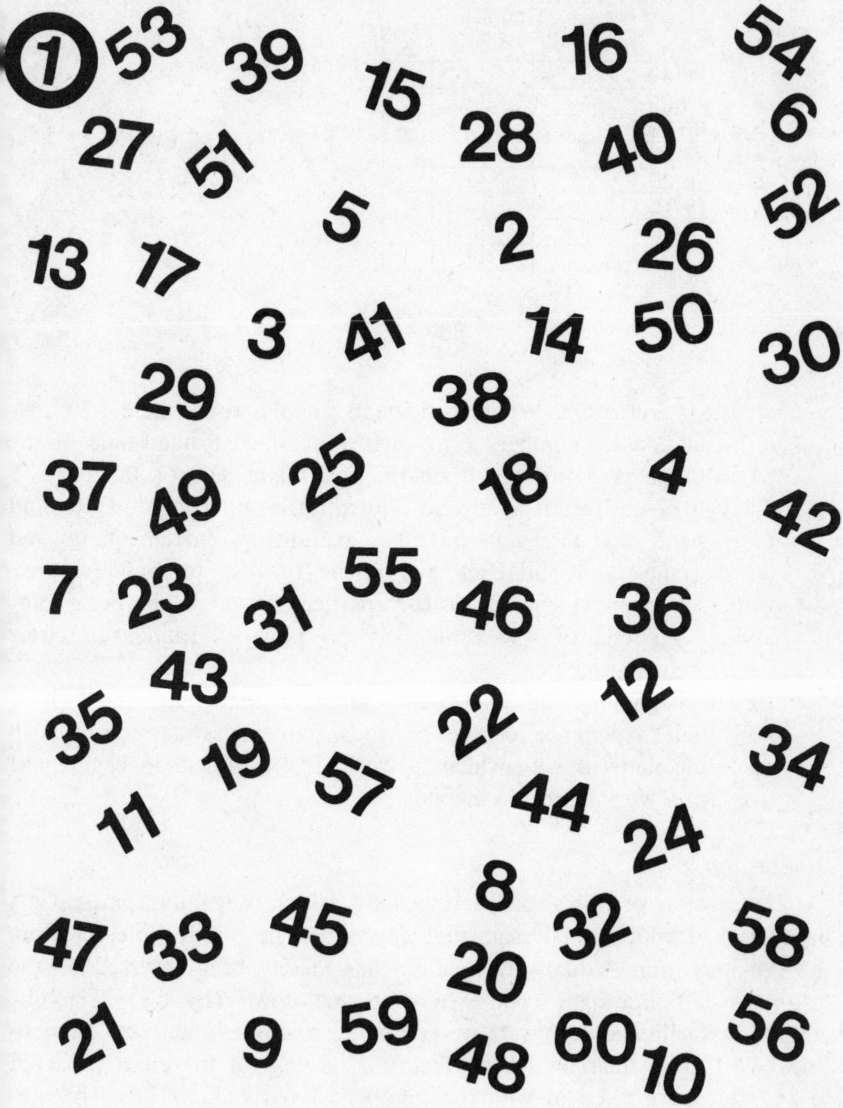

Fig. 11.2

page with the bottom of the page. What participants should notice is that all odd numbers appear on the top half of the page. This knowledge should facilitate their activity on the following round. When you are sure all participants have observed the pattern, ask them to turn to page three and begin work, again, for 45 seconds.

6. Before turning to page four, ask participants to take their booklets —using the page they have just completed—and fold them (without

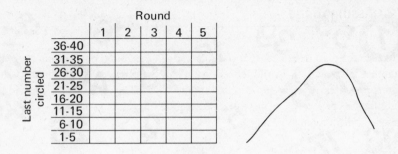

Fig. 11.3

creasing) *vertically.* What participants should notice here is a pattern that locates numbers *1* through *4* on the left-hand side of the page, numbers *5* through *8* on the right-hand side of the page, *9* through *12* on the left-hand side, and so forth on through *60.* Remind participants that they now have two patterns of movement, up and down (odd-even) and back and forth (by 4's) to facilitate their work-on the next round. Instruct participants to begin page four, and at the end of 45 seconds—as on previous rounds—to circle the last number located.

7. Before beginning the final page, reiterate that participants have now their experience of the previous four pages as well as two operating patterns with which to work. Instruct them to begin page five, again working for 45 seconds.

Discussion:

Discussion of this exercise is usually self-starting after participants have worked with a final page that *appears* to be totally different from the previous four. Actually the pattern has merely been reversed on the last page—left and right (odd-even); up and down (by 6's). The discussion is facilitated however, by compiling a crude frequency distribution based upon their own performance. The cells of the chart provided in Fig. 11.3 are filled in with the number of participants in each category. Completion of the chart will allow drawing of a rough "learning curve" that should show an increase in performance over the first four pages, and a drastic drop in round five.

Guide questions might include: What happened? Why did your performance fall off? How many of you looked for the re-occuring patterns? Are they still there? What seem to be the effects of change upon performance? Can such circumstances be anticipated? How could one take advantage of such a situation? Can people be prepared for change? Can you cite personal examples of how change has affected your behavior in much the same way as it did in this exercise?

12. Assumptions

This exercise is designed to raise questions regarding perception and the manner in which it is influenced by past experience. Additionally, this game provides a basis for discussing the impact of groups on individual judgmental processes. The exercise requires about 10 minutes and can be used with any size group.

Procedure:

1. Cover all numbers presented in the attached list in Fig. 12.1 initially, using a flip chart or overhead projector with a cover sheet.
2. Reveal the numbers one at a time and ask participants to add the numbers out loud as they are uncovered.
3. After all of the numbers have been uncovered, most participants will arrive at a total of 6000 rather than 5100.

Discussion:

What factors led to the incorrect conclusions? How significant is the role of past experience in our thinking and behavior in general? In what manner do expectations determine the nature of our experiences?

$$
\begin{array}{r}
1000 \\
1000 \\
20 \\
1000 \\
40 \\
1000 \\
30 \\
1000 \\
10 \\
\hline
\end{array}
$$

Fig. 12.1

13. Observations and Inferences

This exercise focuses on observation and inference. The activity requires approximately 45 minutes and can be used with groups of any size.

Procedure:

1. Worksheets as shown in Fig. 13.1 are distributed, one per participant.
2. Each individual is asked to read the short story at the top of the sheet.
3. Each participant, without consulting others, is then asked to mark each of the 10 statements either "True", or "False", or "?" based upon the information provided in the story. (T is circled if the statement is true, F for statements that are false, and ? for statements where not enough information is provided in the story to be certain whether the statement is true or false.)
4. Participants may refer back to the story as often as they like.

OBSERVATIONS, ASSUMPTIONS, AND INFERENCES WORKSHEET

A businessman had just turned off the lights in the store when a man appeared and demanded money. The owner opened a cash register. The contents of the cash register were scooped up, and the man sped away. A member of the police force was notified promptly.

Based on the story above, are the following statements True, False, or ?

T	F	?	1.	A man appeared after the owner had turned off his store lights.
T	F	?	2.	The robber was a man.
T	F	?	3.	The man did not demand money.
T	F	?	4.	The man who opened the cash register was the owner.
T	F	?	5.	The store-owner scooped up the contents of the cash register and ran away.
T	F	?	6.	Someone opened a cash register
T	F	?	7.	After the man who demanded the money scooped up the contents of the cash register, he ran away.
T	F	?	8.	While the cash register contained money, the story does not state how much.
T	F	?	9.	The robber demanded money of the owner.
T	F	?	10.	The story concerns a series of events in which only three persons are referred to: the owner of the store, a man who demanded money, and a member of the police force.

Fig. 13.1

OBSERVATIONS, ASSUMPTIONS AND INFERENCES WORKSHEET KEY

1. ___?___ The story does not state that the person who turned off the lights was the owner.
2. ___?___ The story does not state that the man who demanded money was a robber. He might, for example, have been a teenage son needing money for a date, a bill collector, or a person collecting for a needy charity.
3. ___F___ The story states that a man did demand money.
4. ___?___ The story does not state that the owner was a male.
5. ___?___ The story does not eliminate the possibility that it was the owner who scooped up the contents of the cash register. Also, the story does not state whether the man "ran" away or not. He may have "sped" away in a car or on a motorcycle.
6. ___T___ The story states that someone opened a cash register.
7. ___?___ The story does not indicate definitely whether the man who demanded money was the same one who scooped up the contents of the cash register. Also, the story does not say he ran away.
8. ___?___ The story does not say the cash register contained money. It might, for example, have contained checks, money orders, keys, or marijuana.
9. ___?___ The story does not say that the man who demanded money was a robber.
10. ___?___ Since the story does not state whether the owner and the businessman were one and the same, there could be either 3 or 4 persons referred to.

Fig. 13.2

5. After all group members have completed the 10 statements, they are asked to indicate by a show of hands how they marked each of the statements. Their responses are tallied on a blackboard or flip chart, in order that each member can compare his answer with those of the other individuals in the group.
6. For each question, volunteers from the group are asked to explain why they selected the answer they did, and to answer questions from others in the group who selected a different answer.
7. At an appropriate time the answers provided on the Worksheet Key, shown in Fig. 13.2 can be provided to the group. This can be done as a part of the discussion of each statement or at the conclusion of debate on all 10 statements.

Discussion:

The discussion following the exercise should deal with the "errors" made in the exercise and explore the extent to which inadequate communication occurring in this activity is typical of communication problems in everyday situations.

What assumptions affected the way group members marked statements T, F, or ?. What aspects of the story contributed to making faulty assumptions? What precautions can be taken to avoid making incorrect assumptions and inferences? Do our assumptions about other people influence the way we talk to and listen to them? What are the origins of such assumptions?

14. Predicting Attitudes

The following exercise can be used to examine the criteria people use in forming opinions and making assumptions about other people and their orientation toward certain topics. It is also useful in raising questions concerning the accuracy and source of those criteria.

Procedure:

1. Use yourself or pick someone out of the group to be used as the focal point.
2. Have the group choose several topics to use as attitude prediction items. (ie. marijuana, women's liberation, etc.)
3. Reproduce the scale given in Fig. 14.1 on a blackboard or flip chart, explaining that 1 indicates an extremely unfavorable attitude while 7 is the most favorable.
4. Using a separate scale for each topic, have members indicate how they would predict that the volunteer would mark the scale for each of the topics.
5. Record participants' choices.
6. After all predictions are recorded have subject tell how he feels concerning the topics.

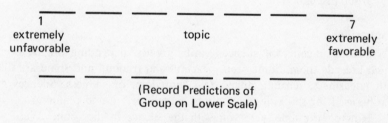

Fig. 14.1

Discussion:

How accurate were individuals' perceptions of others' attitudes? What information was used? To what extent were the predictions reflective of attitudes of the predictors? Why?

15. Silence

This exercise is designed to heighten awareness of the role of silence in human communication, and to highlight differences between individuals in terms of their tolerance for prolonged periods with no verbal exchange.

Procedure:

1. Divide the group into subgroups, A and B. If possible the teams or groups should be visually distinguishable from one another. Armbands, colored ribbons, name tags, or the equivalent are suitable.
2. Ask Team B to leave the room.
3. Inform Team A to be standing when Team B re-enters the room. As Team B enters, Team A members are to nod a greeting, find a chair and sit down, without speaking.
4. Instruct Team B members to re-enter the room, nod a greeting to the Team A members, find a chair, and sit down, without speaking.
5. Regroup the two teams.
6. After three to five minutes of silence (depending upon the tolerance level of the group) ask that the members of Team B leave the room *when they are ready.*
7. After discussion by Team A and B individually, regroup for total group discussion.

Discussion:

The significance of silences varies greatly, depending on the events which precede them. Some seem peaceful and tranquil and some are filled with uneasiness, tension, anger, fear, boredom, or sadness. Silences can also be used for thinking, meditating, contemplating and planning.

How comfortable were you with the silence in the room? Were you content as you waited? What were your expectations? Why? Were you planning to say something? Why? Why not? Team B, were you ready to leave as soon as you were given the option? Who wanted to stay longer? If you were uncomfortable, were you aware of any physical manifestations of this discomfort?

In many countries considerable time may pass before words are exchanged at group meetings. In Japan it is not uncommon for a person engaged in conversation to shut his eyes and think silently for several minutes before responding to a question. In North America we tend to speak more quickly and jump in before the other person has finished his remarks. What is your personal style for dealing with silence in communicating with others.

16. Personal Space

This activity is designed to draw awareness to the nonverbal dimension of personal space. What is the circumference of the space around me which I think of as "mine?" The exercise can be used with any number of persons and requires 10 to 15 minutes.

Procedure:

1. During a discussion *in which participants are standing in dyads,* have one or more people stroll through the room measuring the distance between the speakers with a string.
2. Measurements should be made from shoulder to shoulder; if participants are standing at an angle, take the measurement from the center of one chest to the other. Give each couple their measured piece of string to hold.
3. As the discussion nears an end, ask the participants to draw their string line on a flip chart and write their names at either end of the line. Note the persons who were standing the farthest from each other and those who were closest.
4. When this has been done ask group members to meet again in dyads. Instructions at this point are: "Please meet your partner again, and this time try to decrease the distance between you. How close can you come to each other, still continuing your conversation, without having one person step back? Discuss your feelings about this exercise while standing as close as you can for three minutes."
5. After three minutes have passed call time. "Now take another measure of the space between you and draw it under your original line on the chart with another color maker. Is there a difference?"
6. The activity may be repeated at this time, asking participants to stand farther apart than in the original measurement and explore their reactions to this variation.

Discussion:

Interpersonal spatial relationships vary greatly from culture to culture and within a single culture according to psychological and sociological conditions. What does this exercise say about your use of personal space? How did you feel standing so close to somebody who was not a lover or a relative? Can you describe the feeling? How big is the bubble you "own" or "guard" around you? What point is too close? At what point did you feel your personal space has been invaded? Looking at the flip charts, who was able to come the closest? How did they feel? Do they come from the same ethnic background as you? Did you notice a difference in the personal space between male and male, and male and female? Between adult and child, between child and child? Would it be different for a boss and a best friend? Would the subject matter of conversation make a difference in how close you were standing? What other factors might influence the nature of personal space requirements?

17. Paralanguage

This game focuses on the use of paralanguage to show that tone of voice can be a mode of communicating feeling without the use of recognized vocabulary. Any number of participants can be involved. The exercise requires approximately ten minutes per group.

Procedure:

1. Have participants divide into groups of two to four persons each.
2. Have individuals attempt communication verbally without using recognized words. This may be done facing one another or with participants unable to see one another (back-to-back). (Several small groups may work simultaneously, making sure though that the noise level of the room won't defeat the purpose of the exercise.)

Discussion:

What types of information could be effectively conveyed through paralanguage? (i.e. emotions, directions, etc.) How well were participants able to interpret the sounds of their partner? How can this exercise be helpful in understanding everyday interactions?

18. Eye Contact Patterns

The goal of this exercise is to heighten awareness of the importance of eye contact in interpersonal communication. It requires about fifteen minutes and can be used with groups of any size.

Procedure:
1. Divide the group into two subgroups, A and B. If possible the teams or groups should be visually distinguishable from one another. Armbands, colored ribbons, or a suitable equivalent.
2. Ask Team B to leave the room.
3. Inform Team A that they are to try to influence the members of Team B by saying that they stand to gain by establishing a health clinic in their community.
4. Instruct Team B members that when a Team A participant approaches, they are to avoid all eye contact. It is permissible to talk with them, but not to look them straight in the eye.
5. Bring the two groups together and allow five minutes for interaction.
6. Divide again into subgroups for a short discussion period and then regroup for more in-depth discussion.

Discussion:
Eye contact patterns vary greatly depending on age, sex, social status, social situation, subject matter, cultural background, etc. Traditions about looking others straight in the eye vary from one culture to the next. In Italy men can stare at women, but nice women generally are not to look back. In the Middle East when two people speak they tend to maintain eye contact for long periods of time. North Americans feel less comfortable with prolonged eye contact because of the intimacy implied. In some countries, younger people avoid looking older people in the eye out of respect, and so on.

Norms for the duration of a glance also differ both intra- and interculturally. How did the members of Team A and B feel during the exercise? Did Team A feel rejected, ignored, angry, powerless, involved? How easy was it for Team B to refrain from looking at Team A? How important is eye contact in interpersonal communication? Under what conditions is it especially critical? How does the pattern of eye contact differ according to social situations, the ages of individuals involved, between males and females, when a boss talks to a subordinate, between the punished and the punisher?

19. Situational Geography

The purpose of this exercise is to foster awareness as to the manner in which a physical setting may affect communication processes. The exercise can be utilized with 10–40 participants and requires approximately 30 minutes.

Procedure:

1. Arrange seating positions in the room so as to have all participants seated around a large table except for a few who are seated outside of the group.
2. Conduct a group meeting as usual.
3. Discuss the impact of physical location on participation in group processes.

Discussion:

How did members around the table react? How did the isolates react? Were attempts made to overcome the physical setting? How long did it take participants around the large table to become concerned about the others? Discuss. How can this experience be applied to everyday experiences?

20. Kinesics

The following exercise is designed to focus upon and highlight the importance of nonverbal communication. The activity requires approximately 20 minutes and can be used with 10 to 30 participants. Participants should be seated in a circle facing one another with no barriers to vision between them.

Basically, the activity consists of passing a pair of sticks (or pencils or pens) around the circle of participants in a clockwise direction. The sticks are passed from person to person in either a crossed or uncrossed position—crossed if the passer's legs are crossed, uncrossed if his legs are not crossed.

When the activity begins, only the facilitator knows the correct basis for determining whether the sticks are to be passed crossed or uncrossed. The task of the individuals in the group is to discover the basis upon which the sticks are to be passed correctly. When a person passes the sticks incorrectly (either he passes them crossed when his legs are uncrossed, or uncrossed when his legs are crossed) the facilitator informs him that he is wrong and he corrects himself (although he may not know what the correction means). The facilitator, of course, does not inform the participant of the basis upon which he has made a wrong move.

Procedure:
1. The facilitator passes the sticks to the individual on his left saying: "I pass the sticks uncrossed (assuming his legs are uncrossed)."
2. The person on his left says: "I received the sticks uncrossed (this is merely a repetition of the statement of the previous passer) and pass them uncrossed." If his legs were crossed, the facilitator would say: "That's incorrect," and the individual would instead say that he would "pass them crossed."
3. The process continues until most people in the group have discovered the basis upon which the facilitator tells them they are correct or incorrect. Participants who discover the solution would be asked not to share their answer with others.
4. The exercise may be terminated at the discretion of the facilitator.

Discussion:
Interestingly, most participants assume the pattern they are looking for is a verbal or numerical one. Even though the nonverbal pattern which will give them the solution to the problem is a rather obvious one, it will take most participants considerable amount of time to discover it.

Why did it take so long to determine the correct pattern? What was the reaction of participants as they discovered the correct strategy? What was the reaction of participants who were unable to discover the pattern until quite late in the game? How important are nonverbal cues for understanding others? Discuss. What sorts of things can one get clues about from paying attention to nonverbal communication?

Bibliography

Allport, Gordon W., *Personality and Social Encounter,* Boston: Beacon Press, 1960.

Barnlund, Dean C., *Interpersonal Communication,* Boston: Houghton Mifflin, 1968.

Berlo, David Kenneth, *The Process of Communication,* New York: Holt, Rinehart, and Winston, 1960.

Bettinghaus, E., *Persuasive Communication,* New York: Holt, Rinehart and Winston, 1968.

Bierstedt, John W., Herbert Passin, and Robert K. McKnight, *In Search of Identity,* Minneapolis: University of Minnesota Press, 1958.

Bois, J. S., *The Art of Awareness,* Dubuque, Iowa: W. C. Brown, 1970.

Borden, George A., *An Introduction to Human Communication Theory,* Dubuque, Iowa: W. C. Brown, 1971.

Boulding, Kenneth, *The Image,* Ann Arbor: University of Michigan Press, 1960.

Brown, Roger W., *Words and Things,* New York: Free Press, 1958.

Budd, Richard W. and Brent D. Ruben, *Approaches to Human Communication,* New York: Spartan Books, 1972.

Burke, Kenneth, *Language as Symbolic Action,* Berkeley, California: University of California Press, 1966.

Campbell, James and Hal W. Hepler (eds.), *Dimensions in Communication: Readings,* Belmont, Calif.: Wadsworth, 1970.

Carroll, John B., *Language and Thought,* Englewood Cliffs, N.J.: Prentice-Hall, 1964.

Chase, Stuart, *Power of Words,* New York: Harcourt, Brace, 1954.

Church, J., *Language and the Discovery of Reality,* New York: Random House, 1961.

Dance, Frank E. X., *Human Communication Theory,* New York: Holt, Rinehart and Winston, 1967.

Davitz, Joel R., *The Language of Emotion,* New York: Academic Press, 1969.

DeVito, J. A., *Communication Concepts and Processes,* Englewood Cliffs, N.J.: Prentice-Hall, 1971.

Dorsey, J. M. and W. H. Seegers, *Living Consciously,* Detroit: Wayne State Press, 1959.

Efron, David, *Gesture and Environment,* New York: King's Crown Press, 1941.

Fabun, Don, *Dimensions of Change,* New York: Glencoe Press, 1971.

Goldstein, J. H. and P. E. McGhee, *The Psychology of Humor,* New York: Academic Press.

Hall, Edward T., *The Silent Language,* Garden City, New York: Doubleday, 1959.

Hancock, Alan, *Communication,* New York: Humanities Press, 1971.

Harrison, Randall P., *Beyond Words: An Introduction to Nonverbal Communication,* Englewood Cliffs, N.J.: Prentice-Hall, 1974.

Hayakawa, S. I., *Language in Thought and Action,* New York: Harcourt, Brace, 1939.

Hovland, Carl I, Irving L. Janis, and Harold H. Kelley, *Communication and Persuasion,* New Haven: Yale University Press, 1953.

Johnson, Wendell, *People in Quandaries,* New York: Harper, 1946.

Jourard, Sidney, *The Transparent Self,* New York: Van Nostrand Reinhold, 1968.

Katz, Elihu, and Paul F. Lazarsfeld, *Personal Influence,* New York: Free Press, 1966.

Keltner, John W., *Interpersonal Speech-Communication,* Belmont, California: Wadsworth Publishing Company Inc., 1970.

Kibler, Robert J., and Larry L. Barker, *Conceptual Frontiers in Speech Communication,* New York: Speech Association of America, 1969.

Knapp, Mark L., *Nonverbal Communication in Human Interaction,* New York: Holt, Rinehart and Winston, 1972.

Korzybski, Alfred, *Science and Sanity,* Lakeville, Conn.: The International Non-Aristotelian Library Publishing Company, 1948.

Laing, R. D., H. Phillipson, and A. R. Lee, *Interpersonal Perception,* New York: Springer, 1966.

Laing, R. D., *The Politics of Experience,* London: Penguin Books, 1967.

Lifton, Walter M., *Working with Groups,* New York: Wiley, 1961.

Matson, Floyd and Ashley Montagu, *The Human Dialogue,* New York: Free Press, 1967.

Mehrabian, Albert, *Non-Verbal Communication,* Aldine Publications, 1972.

Mehrabian, Albert, *Silent Messages,* Belmont, Calif.: Wadsworth, 1967.

Miller, Gerald and Michael Burgoon, *New Techniques in Persuasion,* New York: Harper & Row, 1972.

Miller, George A., *Language and Communication,* New York: McGraw-Hill, 1951.

Mortensen, C. David, *Communication: The Study of Human Interaction,* New York: McGraw-Hill, 1972.

Parry, John, *Psychology of Human Communication,* New York: American Elsevier, 1968.

Pierce, J. R., *Symbols, Signals, and Noise,* New York: Harper and Row, Torchbooks, 1961.

Richardson, Lee, *Dimensions of Communication,* New York: Appleton-Century-Crofts, 1969.

Rogers, Carl, *On Becoming a Person,* Boston: Houghton Mifflin, 1961.

Rosenblith, Walter A., *Sensory Communication,* Cambridge: M.I.T. Press, 1961.

Roslansky, John D., *Communication,* New York: Fleet Press, 1969.

Ruben, Brent D. and John Y. Kim, *Human Communication and General Systems Theory,* Rochelle Park, N.J.: Hayden, (in press).

Ruesch, Jurgen and Gregory Bateson, *Communication,* New York: W. W. Norton, 1951, 1968.

Samovar, Larry A. and J. Mills, *Oral Communication,* Dubuque, Iowa: W. C. Brown, 1968.

Schramm, Wilbur, *The Science of Human Communication,* New York: Basic Books, 1963.

Schrank, Jeff, *Communication,* Morristown, N. J.: Silver Burdett, 1970.

Schroder, H. M., M. J. Driver and S. Steufert, *Human Information Processing,* New York: Holt, Rinehart and Winston, 1967.

Sereno, Kenneth K. and C. David Mortensen (eds.), *Foundations of Communication Theory,* New York: Harper, 1970.

Shands, Harley, *Thinking and Psychotherapy,* Cambridge, Mass.: Harvard University Press, 1960.

Shibutani, Tamotsu, *Society and Personality,* Englewood Cliffs, N.J.: Prentice-Hall, 1961.

Smith, Raymond G., *Speech-Communication,* New York: Harper & Row, 1970.

Sommer, R., *Personal Space,* Englewood Cliffs, N.J.: Prentice-Hall, 1969.

Stewart, Daniel K., *The Psychology of Communication,* New York: Funk and Wagnalls, 1969.

Thayer, Lee, *Communication and Communication Systems,* Homewood, Ill.: Richard D. Irwin, 1968.

Toffler, A., *Future Shock,* New York: Random House, 1970.

Vickers, G., *The Art of Judgment,* London: Chapman-Hall, 1965.

Watson, O. M., *Proxemic Behavior,* The Hague: Mouton, 1970.

Watzlawick, Paul, Janet H. Beavin, and Don D. Jackson, *Pragmatics of Human Communication,* New York: W. W. Norton & Company, 1967.

Weaver, Carl H., *Human Listening,* Indianapolis, Indiana: Bobbs-Merrill, 1972.

Weinberg, Harry L., *Levels of Knowing and Existence,* New York: Harper and Row, 1959.

Whorf, B. L. *Language, Thought, and Reality,* Cambridge, Mass.: M.I.T. Press, 1956.

Weiner, N., *The Human Use of Human Beings,* New York: Avon, 1950.

Young, J. Z., *Doubt and Certainty in Science,* New York: Oxford University Press, 1950.

Part 2
SOCIAL COMMUNICATION

Communication is the *sine qua non* and sustaining lifeblood of social organization. Whether in interpersonal, small groups, or institutional contexts, social communication is the process which gives life to and perpetuates multi-person units.

The process is generic, abstract, and difficult to grasp in theory and often frustrating, ambiguous and difficult to cope with in practice. It is through social communication that norms, rules, standards, ethics, knowledges, values, and the like are defined and transferred from individual to individual and from one generation to the next. And it is also as a consequence of particular social communication phenomena that social change comes about.

The activities included in this section provide insight into a variety of dimensions which are critical to social communication and social organization. Included are exercises on rumor, serial information transfers, feedback, prediction and interpersonal perception, behavior differences, group reactions to individual members, group formation, interpersonal credibility, cooperative and competitive communication, communication and trust, minority and majority communication, group problem solving, group initiation and membership, group decision making, and leadership.

The bibliography suggests a number of relevant readings; familiarity with the concepts presented in those sources is critical to effective utilization of the simulations and games described. It is also suggested that where possible several participants serve as observers and reporters as described in Part 4.

21. Rumor: Serial Transmission of Information

This simulation serves as a basis for examining the process of information transfer between individuals. Additionally, it is useful for indicating how many various assumptions, inferences, observations, expectations, and information categorizing, ordering, and storing are involved in social communication. The activity also is useful as a basis for presenting the concept of rumor and for demonstrating the unreliability of second-hand information. The exercise requires about 45 minutes and can be used with a group of any size.

Procedure:

1. Four or more participants are asked to leave the room.
2. An action picture or film is presented to the remaining participants.
3. One of the participants who was exposed to the presentation is selected to provide a first-hand account of what he saw.
4. The selected participant begins by telling the group what he saw. They can correct him as necessary.
5. The first of those who left the room (participant No. 2) is called back in and is asked to be seated at the front of the room. He is then told about the contents of the film or picture by the participant who was present for the actual viewing (participant No. 1).
6. Depending upon the concepts to be emphasized, participant No.2 may be allowed to ask questions of participant No. 1 (feedback), or he may be prevented from doing so. *Use of written notes should be prohibited.*
7. The group at large observes the information transfer process, and does not comment or question participants in the information chain.
8. Participant No. 3 is asked to enter the room and be seated next to Participant No. 2 at the front of the room. The description of the content of the original presentation is passed along by No. 2 to No. 3, who will subsequently pass it along to No. 4 when he is called into the room.
9. The process continues until all individuals who were excluded from the original presentation have become part of the information transfer chain.
10. The last person in the chain then repeats back to the entire group what he understands to be the content of the picture or film.

Discussion:

The film may be reshown before or after discussion. In some instances it may be useful to reshow the presentation more than once, to make the point that even when a person has a chance to experience something twice or three times, he is still unable to perceive and store all of the information which may be present.

The primary focus of the activity, however, is upon the process of transmitting information in serial fashion. Typically three kinds of errors occur: Levelling, Sharpening, and Assimilation. Levelling refers to dropping of details, sharpening to the emphasizing of particular—often unimportant—points, and assimilation to the distortion of some points and the addition of others which were not present in the original event.

Video or audio tape recording of the communication chain is useful for stimulating discussion of the process of information transfer.

Where the equipment is not available, the instructor may wish to lead the group in a discussion of the specific errors that occurred as the message moved from person to person.

What factors seem to contribute to breakdowns of information as it passes from one individual to another? Discuss. What techniques seemed to be useful in avoiding breakdowns? How reliable is second-hand information? Was what occurred typical of what happens in everyday social communication? What can be done to avoid the problems of acting upon incorrect second-hand information? Discuss. Are some people more reliable as sources of information than others? How do you decide who is and who isn't? Do factors such as their sex, age, or color make a difference to how believable individuals are perceived to be?

22. Feedback

This exercise is useful for introducing the concept of *feedback* (information fed-back to a communicator that helps assess how he was interpreted by his receivers). The concept is important to understanding how human communication works, and for improving one's ability to function effectively in social interaction. This exercise requires approximately 30 minutes, and can be used with a group of any size.

Procedure:

1. Select a pictogram as provided in Figs. 22.1–22.4.
2. Select one participant to sit at the front of the room. Provide him with the sheet of paper on which the selected pictogram is illustrated.
3. The chosen participant is instructed that his task is to attempt to communicate orally everything the other participants need to know in order to reproduce the pictogram on the blank sheet of paper with which each has been provided.
4. The audience participants cannot, of course, see the original pictogram, and the chosen communicator is not allowed to use gestures.

Fig. 22.1

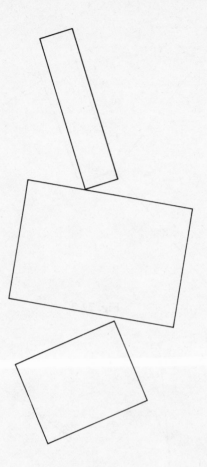

Fig. 22.2

5. The participants *are not* allowed to ask questions.
6. Instructor may wish to record the amount of time that the chosen individual requires to provide instructions to the audience participants.
7. When the communicator has finished, the audience participants are shown the original pictogram, and the instructor computes a rough percentage of those participants who reproduced the figure correctly, noting the amount of time elapsed during the activity.
8. The process is repeated a second time, using a different pictogram, with either the same or a different person providing instructions to the other participants.
9. This time, however, audience participants *are* allowed to ask questions.

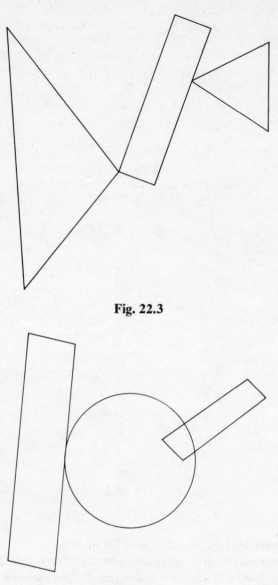

Fig. 22.3

Fig. 22.4

10. Once again the instructor may wish to record elapsed time and calculate the percentage of participants who were able to reproduce the figure on their paper.

Discussion:

With few exceptions, the cycle of the exercise without audience feedback, will take less time, but result in fewer correct reproductions of the figure. This can serve as the basis for a discussion of the relative merits of *efficiency* or speed in communication versus *effectiveness*. The exercise also serves to underscore the imprecision of language and the difficulty of describing one's personal experience to others in a manner that leads to identical understanding by them.

What are the advantages of feedback in this exercise? What kinds of feedback worked best? Questions? moans? groans? snickers? What communication problems occurred in the exercise? Are there certain techniques for communicating to the audience that seemed to work better than others? What are typical examples of the uses of feedback in everyday communication? Can feedback be non-verbal as well as verbal? Discuss. How can feedback be used effectively in social communication?

23. Prediction and Interpersonal Perception

This activity is designed to focus upon the processes involved in making and reacting to first impressions. Particular emphasis is placed upon non-verbal aspects of impressions and the assumptions which are made as a consequence. The exercise can be used with any number of dyads and requires 10 to 15 minutes.

Procedure:

1. Participants are asked to select someone in the room with whom they are not acquainted, but would like to get to know.
2. Persons are asked to approach the chosen individual and share with the other the basis as to why they selected one another. Here the discussion may focus on any verbal or non-verbal messages which were transmitted or received. Participants also share with their dyad partner their first impressions of one another and the kinds of assumptions they had made based upon these impressions. How valid were they? Participants are asked to explore this issue. Allow three to five minutes.
3. Following this discussion, ask each dyad partner to make three predictions about the other member of the dyad: 1. What kind of music he or she likes best? 2. What his or her favorite sport is? 3. What are his or her favorite foods?
4. After each person has had a chance to guess, participants should check the validity and accuracy of their guesses with each other. Allow three to five minutes.

Discussion:

As we see other people we tend to size them up, draw assumptions, and make predictions. Are these assumptions accurate? How far off are they? What kinds of signals do we tend to give off to others during an initial meeting? To what extent do we have control over them? How important are the verbal cues we give off in comparison to the non-verbal cues with regard to the impressions others get of us? When participants checked through their assumptions with their partners, how close were they? What kinds of rationales were used for what he or she liked best? Was it body build, muscle tone, hair style, amount of make-up (for a woman), choice of clothes style and color, age? What stereotypes were reinforced or altered as a result of the exercise?

24. Behavior Differences

This exercise is designed to focus upon one's own behavior style and the work styles of others. The goal is to enhance awareness and acceptance of differences between individuals and to provide a basis for productive confrontations among individuals when styles clash during small group work. The activity can be used with up to 40 participants within approximately 40 minutes to one hour.

Procedure:

1. Ask the group to develop a list of some of the ways in which individuals differ in discussion or small work groups, creating a list of opposites also.
2. Have the group choose one of the pair-categories to discuss and divide themselves into two groups on the basis of the extent to which the words describe their own behavior.
3. Rearrange the two groups into two circles—an inner and outer circle.
4. Have the inner group discuss why they act as they do, making sure that each member discusses his own behavior and not the behavior of the group. After everyone has spoken or had the chance to express him or herself, ask the outer group to discuss how they feel about those who behave the opposite way.
5. At the end of the second discussion, have the groups switch places and repeat the process.

Discussion:

What can be learned about others who behave differently? How did members from opposite groups react to the reasons given during the discussions? How can this information lead to improve the small group interactions?

25. Group-to-One Feedback

This exercise is designed to give participants useful feedback concerning how others see them. It can be used with small to intermediate size groups ranging from 7-40 participants and requires from 30 minutes to several hours, depending upon how long participants desire to continue.

Procedure:
1. Have a group member volunteer for the exercise.
2. Ask the group to think about what kind of car they imagine the volunteer as, were he a car. (Other topics such as dogs they would own or types of houses they would live in can be used as substitutes.) Have members describe the car and why they chose that model as characteristic of the subject.
3. Allow as many volunteers as possible to participate.

Discussion:
How was this type of feedback dealt with by volunteers? By the group? Was interpersonal feedback accepted more under these conditions than had it been more direct? Why? Was direct feedback offered more freely under these conditions? Why? How can this exercise be useful in normal interactions? Did the descriptions provide more information about the individual being described or the describer?

26. Group Formation

This exercise creates an interaction among individuals, and is useful as a means of exploring the processes of group formation. The exercise requires 15–30 minutes and can be used with any number of participants.

Procedure:
1. Have participants arrange themselves about the room.
2. Place a ball of yarn on floor, telling members they are to pass the ball of yarn to someone else in the room, with whom they would like to interact, holding on to the yarn after passing it.
3. Continue the exercise until all have received and passed the yarn and are holding on to it.

Discussion:
Describe the group process involved in passing the yarn. Were all participants involved? Discuss. How were individual feelings manifested in behavior? How did the activity affect the individuals feeling toward others in the group? Is the group more or less cohesive as a consequence of the activity?

27. Grouping

This exercise serves as a basis for exploring individual reactions to being grouped, as well as providing participants with the opportunity to discover similarities and differences between group members. The exercise can be utilized with any number of participants and requires approximately 45 minutes.

Procedure:
1. In an empty room randomly group in different-sized clusters (3 to 6 chairs per group).
2. Prepare room by placing nametags on chairs.
3. Have participants enter the room and instruct them to find their proper places.
4. Inform these groups that their initial task is to discover why they were grouped as they were.
5. Allow adequate time for groups to arrive at a consensus.
6. Have each group report its conclusions.

Discussion:
What feelings were fostered by the exercise? What procedures did the group follow in reaching conclusions? In general, what are the consequences of being categorized? What is communicated by the categories? In what sense does this activity relate to "real life" problems?

28. Communicator Credibility

This exercise is useful for raising questions about the importance of status and roles upon outcomes in the communication process. The exercise requires approximately an hour and can be utilized with any number of participants.

Procedure:

1. Tell the participants that they will take part in an experimental learning situation.
2. Divide the group into thirds sending each third to a different room to hear a speech on the subject of civil disobedience.
3. Introduce the speaker to the first group by telling them he is a minister. After he has finished with the first group introduce the same speaker to the second group as a member of the police force, and to the third group as a member of a liberation movement. To each group the guest presents the identical speech.
4. Have groups fill out a written attitude survey concerning the speech.
5. Re-group all of the participants and discuss the topic briefly.
6. Tell the participants the person's true identity after the discussion.

Discussion:

What effects did the differing titles have on the three groups' perceptions? How did they affect the judgments of the speaker? the speech? What were the reactions to finding out that others were perceiving the person differently?

29. Cooperative and Competitive Communication

This exercise is designed to highlight some of the important elements of cooperative and competitive communication between individuals within a group. The activity is designed for use with a number of groups of five participants each, and requires approximately 45 minutes. Each group of participants should be seated around a table.

Procedure:

1. Each group of five participants is given a packet consisting of five envelopes containing materials illustrated in Fig. 29.1.

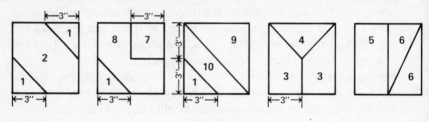

Fig. 29.1

2. Each group is told that its task is to construct five equal-size squares utilizing the materials in the envelopes.
3. They may proceed in any manner they choose observing the following rules: 1) *no talking or gesturing;* 2) participants may give pieces to other group members, but they *cannot take pieces* from other members; 3) participants may not pool all the pieces of the group into a single pile, nor may they contribute pieces to a central pool. All pieces given by a participant must be given to a specific person in the group.

Discussion:

How closely were the rules followed? Which ones were broken? Why? Were group members competitive or cooperative? To what extent? Was there a change as the task progressed? Once an individual had completed a small square was he content to withdraw from the task, even though others had not yet been successful in completing squares? Discuss. How willing were people to give up puzzle pieces? Was it possible to not communicate? Were there ways in which the group could have completed the five squares more rapidly? What are some of the parallels between the things that happened in this exercise and things which occur in society?

Exercise Materials

Each group of five individuals will need a packet consisting of five envelopes. Each envelope will contain puzzle pieces which, when properly matched with pieces from other envelopes, will form five equal squares.

To construct the packet, begin with five 6-inch cardboard squares. Mark them as indicated below and cut along indicated lines. Note that all puzzle pieces marked with the same number should be of equal size, such that they are interchangeable with all other pieces labeled the same number. All number 1 pieces for example, must be the same size. Mark numbers in pencil so that they can be erased prior to use in an exercise.

Label each of five envelopes A, B, C, D, and E. Sort the labeled pieces and place them into the envelopes in the following pattern.

Envelope	Puzzle Piece Number
A	9, 8, 5
B	1, 1, 1, 3
C	1, 10
D	4, 6
E	7, 2, 6, 3

Erase the penciled puzzle piece numbers and label the pieces with the letter designating the appropriate envelope. This will facilitate reassembling of envelopes after use.

30. Trust

This game focuses upon cooperation and competition, intergroup trust and the consequences of breaching trust. The total time required to complete the operations varies between 45 minutes and an hour. The exercise is conducted with two teams of not more than eight members each.

Procedure:

1. The instructor forms two teams, the Red team and the Blue team, seated far enough apart so that they will not overhear each other or disrupt each other's deliberations. The teams should be told not to communicate with each other except when instructed to do so.

2. Score sheets are distributed to all participants with the following verbal instructions:

   a. The teams will participate in 10 rounds of decision making with the Red team choosing either an A or B and the Blue team choosing either an X or Y each round.

   b. The choice of one letter or the other should be made round by round, since each decision is a separate one frequently dependent upon past choices as well as being interdependent upon the choice of the opposing team.

   c. The following combinations of choices will result in the following point assignments:

Choices		Point Assignment	
Red	*Blue*	*Red*	*Blue*
A	X	+3	+3
A	Y	–6	+6
B	X	+6	–6
B	Y	–3	–3

   d. Points are cumulative throughout the game.

3. The facilitator signals the beginning of Round 1, instructing each team that it has three minutes to arrive at a decision. At the end of the round the instructor directs each group to write its group decision on a piece of paper which is collected as nearly simultaneously as possible.

4. The instructor announces the two choices and posts the choices and resultant scores on a large tally sheet (previously drawn on a blackboard or flip chart).

5. Rounds 2 and 3 are conducted in the same manner, three minutes each with scores posted after each round.

6. Before beginning Round 4, the instructor points out, because it is a special round (the scores are *doubled* for this round), that each

team is to select a representative to meet and talk with one another prior to the beginning of the round. The discussion of the two representatives should be a private one; the instructor allows three minutes for the conference. At the end of the deliberations, the representatives return to their groups and round 4 is begun. At the end of this round the resultant scores are doubled and posted.

7. Rounds 5, 6, 7, and 8 proceed in the same manner as Rounds 1–3.
8. Before the beginning of Round 9, the instructor announces that Rounds 9 and 10 are special rounds since the scores for these two rounds are *squared* (note that only the scores are squared; the signs do not change as they would in normal mathematical operations involving the squaring of a negative number. For purposes of this exercise a −3 squared will equal a −9). Another conference is held. Groups may use the same or a different representative who will, as before, meet privately for a three minute discussion. At the end of the round, the resultant scores (this time squared) are posted.
9. Round 10 proceeds just as Round 1 did except that the scores are, as in Round 9, squared. This fact should be known to participants prior to the meeting of the representatives just before Round 9. There is no meeting before Round 10 (unless the instructor wishes to use this variation).

Discussion:

Prior to opening the discussion, the instructor computes the point total for each team and the sum of the two team scores. He posts this grand total and also posts the *maximum positive* outcome, 90 points (this grand total can only be achieved by the two teams remaining in the AX mode throughout the exercise). To start the discussion (or at some appropriate time during) the instructor might wish to subtract the grand total amassed by the two teams from the possible maximum grand total. Specific questions might be: What were the goals of each team? At what point did strategies change? How did the Red team or the Blue team respond to a breach of trust by the other team (if this occurs)? Although there were no discussions preceding 8 of the 10 rounds, was there a means of communication available to the two groups? How did previous choices of the other team influence subsequent decisions? Was everyone in the group agreed on every choice? How was dissent accommodated within the groups? Did either team ever respond to the actions of the other group (laughter, apparent intense discussions, etc.)? What assumptions were made because of certain behaviors of the other group? What did the representatives talk about? Did the group honor agreements arrived upon by the representatives? If not, why not? If so, why did they? How does this exercise relate to your own interpersonal relationships? To relationships of societal groups? To international relationships? What strategies could have been developed to avoid or reinforce certain kinds of decisions? What implications do these have for your own personal behavior?

Other issues which can be discussed as a result of this exercise are effects of trust on relationships, definitions of winning and losing, and the consequences of cooperation or competition.

31. Minority and Majority Communication

The Shoe Game was developed to increase awareness of the processes of communication in discrimination. The activity can be used with 12 to 50 participants and requires approximately 45 minutes.

Procedure:

1. Participants are asked to count off "black, white, black, white," and so on until everyone is so designated.
2. The "blacks" are told to leave the room, while the "whites" stay.
3. "Whites" are then asked to take off their shoes and pile them in the center of the floor.
4. "Blacks" are asked to come back into the room.
5. "Blacks" are told to pair up the shoes, find the owner and put the shoes on his or her feet.
6. The "blacks" are instructed not to talk during this phase of the exercise.

Discussion:

How did it feel to be labeled as either "black" or "white?" Discuss. How did "blacks" feel about being sent out of the room? How did "whites" feel about having someone wait on them? How did "blacks" feel about their role in the exercise? Was the experience embarrassing? In what ways does this exercise parallel majority and minority communication in everyday life?

32. Group Problem-Solving

The following game focuses on group problem-solving, and is designed to illuminate the communication processes involved. The exercise requires approximately one-half hour and can be used with one or more groups of 5 to 8 persons each.

The task itself is an easy one—constructing a simple object such as a checkerboard, a flag, or a coat of arms, using colored construction paper, scissors, glue, pencils, pens, and other materials supplied by the instructor. The use of a task of this sort allows for focusing upon the group communication processes.

Procedure:
1. Participants are seated around a table.
2. An envelope containing construction paper, a pair of scissors, stapler and other minimally necessary materials are placed in the center of the table.
3. Instructions are given to participants in the form of a simple statement: "Using the materials in this envelope, make a checkerboard (or flag, or coat of arms)." A model may be provided by the instructor if he or she wishes.
4. The imposition of a time limit may be appropriate. If so, participants should be informed at this point.
5. Announce when predetermined time span has elapsed, or if none was set, ask participants to inform the instructor when they are finished.

Discussion:

To what extent was the project a *group* effort? Discuss. How did the group make its decisions? Did the group function creatively? How effectively did the group function? How did the group define the problems it decided to deal with? Who were the most influential group members? Ask each participant to express what percentage of the finished product was a result of his or her effort?

33. Group Initiation and Membership

The purpose of this exercise is to explore the feelings of those isolated from the group, concentrating especially on the desire for and attempts of the isolates to become a part of the group as well as the manner in which the group handles them. The exercise requires approximately one-half hour and can be used with 10–30 participants.

Procedure:

1. Ask for a volunteer for the exercise.
2. Have the remainder of the group lock arms to form a circle, telling them they are to keep the volunteer from entering.
3. Tell the volunteer to try to break into the circle.
4. Repeat the process with other volunteers.

Discussion:

How did it feel to be a member of the circle? To be the isolate? To become a member? How were attempts by the isolate to break in dealt with by the group? What parallels can be drawn between participants' actions during the exercise and "normal" group initiation and membership processes?

34. Group Decision Making

This exercise is designed to provide a means for exploring the dynamics of individual and group decision-making, and the processes through which group concensus is reached. The activity requires approximately 45 minutes and can be used with groups of 5 to 10 persons. Each group of participants should be seated in a circle or around a table.

Procedure:
1. Worksheets are distributed, one per participant. See Fig. 34.1
2. Each individual is asked to read and carefully consider the 8 statements about the objectives of education provided in each worksheet.

GROUP DECISION MAKING WORKSHEET

_____ Society is held together by right behavior. Education should teach people to be good, honest, and upright human beings.

_____ Man is happiest when he knows he has done a skillful job. People should be taught things that will help them to do their work better.

_____ Knowledge should be valued for its own sake because in knowledge there is wisdom. Education should teach those things that have been found to be true for all people for all times.

_____ The family is most important. Education should teach one to be a more able and responsible family member.

_____ In these times, when we must all work together to build our country, education must teach us first and foremost to be informed, reliable, and cooperative citizens.

_____ Now after all the talk is over, we must admit that it is natural for men to want a reasonably comfortable way of life and a share of the good things they deserve. Education should primarily be planned to bring a man money and success.

_____ If our nation is to go ahead, our people must start by knowing and understanding their own historical and cultural roots. Education should teach us about our past — what parts of it help and hinder us now.

_____ Freedom means choice. A man with no education may believe all or nothing he hears or reads. But education should teach him how to make intelligent choices in all areas of his life.

Fig. 34.1

3. Each participant, without consulting others, is then asked to rank the statements from 1 to 8, placing a 1 in the blank next to the statement with which he most agrees, a 2 next to the statement he

agrees with next most, and so on through 8, the statement he disagrees with most strongly.

4. After all group members have completed their own individual rankings, the group is given the task of arriving at one overall ranking, from 1–8, of the statements which is agreeable to all members of the group.

5. The group decision making can proceed in whatever manner the group members decide, with two constraints: 1) voting when used as the only means of determining the overall rank, is not permitted; 2) numerical averaging of the individual ranks is not permitted.

6. Alternative lists which can be used in place of Fig. 34.1 are provided in Figs. 34.2 through 34.4

OPTIONAL GROUP DECISION MAKING WORKSHEET

____ ____ Husbands and wives should share equally such tasks as washing the dishes, emptying the garbage, and cooking meals.

____ ____ A woman should be paid the same as a man if she has the same work experiences and is being hired to do the same job.

____ ____ The title "Ms." is the appropriate identification for all women — single and married, just as "Mr." is appropriate for all men.

____ ____ A woman employee should receive time off for having a baby without losing her seniority, just as a male employee is permitted a leave of absence for personal or family reasons.

____ ____ The government should provide centers for taking care of children while their mothers work, in the same way that the government provides support for the highway system, parking ramps and other services related to work.

____ ____ Women and men who do the same job should have exactly the same titles, rather than distinctions like lady-wrestler, stewardess, policeman.

____ ____ Women should be permitted to rise to the highest job positions, including management jobs where they will supervise male employees.

____ ____ Women should be subject to the military draft just as men are.

Fig. 34.2

Discussion:

Probably the most significant aspect of this exercise is the discussion session which follows the activity itself. During that discussion the group may have a tendency to focus upon the content of the exercise—the statements about education. While educational objectives have a wide interest, care should be taken to insure that the discussion centers upon the individual and group interaction and outcomes which occurred quite apart from the specific topics. Process observation guides are useful if it is feasible for several individuals who are not participating in the exercise to observe the working group.

OPTIONAL GROUP DECISION-MAKING WORKSHEET

Which five of the following characteristics are most important for a leader?

1. Well-organized
2. Sense of humor
3. Intelligence
4. Interest in people
5. Patience
6. Physical health and vigor
7. Understands people
8. Fairness
9. Good moral character
10. Doesn't play favorites
11. Open to change
12. Willing to admit mistakes
13. Good leader
14. Respected in community

The five most important characteristics in the list are:

1. _____
2. _____
3. _____
4. _____
5. _____

Fig. 34.3

What methods did the group use in its attempts at decision making? Which methods were most effective? Discuss. How representative is the overall group ranking of the ideas and attitudes of the individual group members? Were some group members more successful in influencing the overall ranking to look like their own ranking, than were other group members? What kind of leadership was present in the group? Democratic? Authoritarian? Was the leadership effective? How much a part of the group decision is felt by the individual group members? How well did the group tolerate opinions which were not consistent with the majority?

OPTIONAL GROUP DECISION MAKING WORKSHEET
RACIAL ATTITUDES

_____ _____ Only a black person can really understand another black.

_____ _____ All administrators of a "Black Studies Program" must be black.

_____ _____ Standards should be lowered to admit any member of a minority group who wants a college education.

_____ _____ Black students ought to be able to have all-black dormitories if they want them.

_____ _____ The most meaningful path to "equal status" is separatism for blacks with things under their own control and direction.

_____ _____ There should be no limit set on the number of black students admitted to any college or university.

_____ _____ It is the responsibility of every white student to do everything he or she can to help the blacks on campus get what they want.

_____ _____ Black students' demands to the college should be presented as "Non-negotiable."

Fig. 34.4

How far are the individual's ranks from the final group ranking? (Subtract individual's rank of each item from group rank—ignoring + or − signs—to arrive at a different score for each group member.) What do these scores reflect?

35. Leadership

The following exercise focuses on desirable leadership characteristics. The exercise requires approximately one hour and can be utilized with any number of participants.

Procedure:

1. Pass out a copy of the leadership characteristics sheet shown in Fig. 35.1 to each participant.
2. Instruct them that they are to select five characteristics which they feel are the most important for a group/community leader and to rank those characteristics. (1 being most important; 5 being least important.)
3. Allow five minutes for this portion of the exercise.
4. After all participants have selected the five most important characteristics, have the group divide themselves into subgroups consisting of 6–8 participants.
5. Instruct participants that they will have 20 minutes to arrive at a group decision as to the five most important characteristics and a rank order for the five.

LEADERSHIP CHARACTERISTICS SHEET

Below is a list of characteristics which might be used to describe a group or community leader. You are to select from this list five characteristics – the ones you feel are the most important for a group leader and to rank the five characteristics in order of importance (1 being most important; 5 least important). List the five characteristics in the order you decide, by placing numbers next to your choice in the space provided. You have five minutes to complete this task.

____ ____ Initiative	____ ____ Generalized experience
____ ____ Interest in people	____ ____ Specialized experience
____ ____ Well organized	____ ____ Sense of humor
____ ____ Awareness of local politics	____ ____ Good socializer
____ ____ Intelligence	____ ____ Respect in community
____ ____ Emotional stability	____ ____ Financial independence
____ ____ Cultural interests	____ ____ Physical health and vigor
____ ____ Loyalty to community	____ ____ Grasp of local issues

---

Fig. 35.1

6. List three rules that must be followed in reaching consensus.

   You must work as a group.

   Do not choose a formal discussion leader.

   Do not take formal votes to reach your decision . . . depend on consensus.

7. Lead discussion concentrating on how in fact, each group operated in reaching their decisions.

Discussion:

How do the group list of characteristics compare to the leadership methods utilized in deriving those lists? Did the group list reflect a large portion of the participants or only a few members? Discuss. How were differences of opinion dealt with? Was consensus reached by active participation or by inactive "agreement"? Discuss. If there were some inactive participators how were they dealt with by the group?

Bibliography

Aranguren, José L., *Human Communication,* New York: McGraw-Hill, 1967.

Argyle, Michael, *Social Interaction,* New York: Atherton, 1969.

Baker, Larry L. and Robert J. Kibler, *Speech Communication Behavior,* Englewood Cliffs, N.J.: Prentice-Hall, 1971.

Barnlund, Dean C., *Interpersonal Communication,* Boston: Houghton Mifflin, 1968.

Bennis, Warren C., *Changing Organizations,* New York: McGraw-Hill, 1966.

Bennis, Warren, E. H. Schein, F. I. Steel, and D. E. Berlew, *Interpersonal Dynamics,* Homewood, Ill.: Dorsey-Irwin, 1968.

Berger, Peter L., and Thomas Luckmann, *The Social Construction of Reality,* New York: Doubleday, 1966.

Bion, W. R., *Experience in Groups,* New York: Basic Books, 1969.

Birdwhistell, Ray L., *Kinesics and Context,* Philadelphia: University of Pennsylvania Press, 1970.

Bormann, E. G. and N. C. Bormann, *Effective Small Group Communication*, Minneapolis, Minn.: Burgess Publishing Co., 1972.

Brooks, William D., *Speech Communication,* Dubuque, Iowa: W. C. Brown, 1971.

Budd, Richard W. and Brent D. Ruben, *Approaches to Human Communication,* New York: Spartan Books, 1972.

Burke, Kenneth, *Language as Symbolic Action,* Berkeley, Calif.: University of California Press, 1966.

Burke Kenneth, *Permanence and Change,* New York: The New Republic, 1935.

Burton, Arthur, *Encounter,* San Francisco, Calif.: Jossey-Bass, 1970.

Campbell, James and Hal W. Hepler, *Dimensions in Communication: Readings,* Belmont, Calif.: Wadsworth Pub. Co., 1970.

Capp, Glen R., *Basic Oral Communication,* Englewood Cliffs, N.J.: Prentice-Hall, 1971.

Carpenter, Edmund S. and Marshall McLuhan, *Explorations in Communication,* Boston: Beacon Press, 1966.

Cathcart, Robert S. and Larry A. Samovar, *Small Group Communication*, Dubuque, Iowa: W. C. Brown, 1970.

Cohen, Joseph, *Group Dynamics,* New York: Rand McNally, 1971.

Dance, Frank E. X., *Human Communication Theory,* New York: Holt, Rinehart and Winston, 1967.

Dance, Frank E. and Carl E. Larson, *Speech Communication,* New York: Holt, Rinehart and Winston, 1972.

DeVitto, Joseph, *Communication,* Englewood Cliffs, N.J.: Prentice-Hall, 1971.

Diedrich, R. C. and H. A. Dye, *Group Procedures: Purposes, Processes and Outcomes,* Boston: Houghton Mifflin, 1972.

Duncan, Hugh Dalziel, *Communication and Social Order,* New York: Oxford University Press, 1969.

Duncan, Hugh Dalziel, *Symbols and Social Theory,* New York: Oxford University Press, 1962.

Duncan, Hugh Dalziel, *Symbols in Society,* New York: Oxford University Press, 1968.

Eisenberg, Abne M. and Ralph R. Smith Jr., *Nonverbal Communication,* Indianapolis, Indiana: Bobbs-Merrill, 1971.

Foote, Nelson S., and L. S. Cottrell, Jr., *Identity and Interpersonal Competence,* Chicago: University of Chicago Press, 1965.

Foundation for Research on Human Behavior, *Communication in Organizations,* Ann Arbor, Mich: University of Michigan Press, 1959.

Frings, H., and M. Frings, *Animal Communication,* New York: Blaisdell, 1964.

Gerth, Hans, and C. Wright Mills, *Character and Social Structure,* New York: Harcourt, Brace, 1953.

Giffin, Kim and Bobby R. Patton, *Fundamentals of Interpersonal Communication,* New York: Harper & Row, 1971.

Goffman, Erving, *Behavior in Public Places,* New York: Free Press, 1963.

Goffman, Erving, *Interaction Ritual,* Garden City, New York: Doubleday, Anchor Books, 1967.

Goffman, Erving, *Strategic Interaction,* Philadelphia: University of Pennsylvania Press, 1969.

Goffman, Erving, *The Presentation of Self in Everyday Life,* Garden City, N.Y.: Doubleday, 1959.

Gordon, George N., *The Language of Communication,* New York: Hastings House, 1969.

Grant, Barbara M., *Moves: An Analysis of Non-Verbal Activity,* New York: Teachers College Press, Columbia University, 1971.

Gulley, Halbert E., *Discussion, Conference and Group Process,* New York: Holt, Rinehart & Winston, 1960.

Hall, Edward T., *The Hidden Dimension,* Garden City, N.Y.: Doubleday, 1966.

Haney, William V., *Communication and Organizational Behavior,* Homewood, Ill.: Richard D. Irwin, 1967.

Heider, Fritz, *The Psychology of Interpersonal Relations,* New York: Wiley, 1958.

Herzberg, Frederick, et al., *The Motivation to Work,* New York: Wiley & Sons, 1959.

Homans, G. C., *The Human Group,* New York: Harcourt, Brace, 1950.

Innis, Harold A., *The Bias of Communication,* Toronto: University of Toronto Press, 1951.

Johnson, Wendell, *People in Quandaries,* New York: Harper, 1946.

Katz, Elihu and Paul F. Lazarsfeld, *Personal Influence,* New York: Free Press, 1955.

Keltner, John W., *Interpersonal Speech-Communication,* Belmont, Calif.: Wadsworth, 1970.

Kibler, Robert J., and Larry L. Barker, *Conceptual Frontiers in Speech,* New York: Speech Association of America, 1969.

Knapp, Mark L., *Nonverbal Communication in Human Interaction,* New York: Holt, Rinehart and Winston, 1972.

Korzybski, Alfred, *Science and Sanity,* Lakeville, Conn.: The International Non-Aristotelian Library Publishing Company, 1948.

Laing, R. D., H. Phillipson, and A. R. Lee, *Interpersonal Perception,* New York: Springer, 1966.

Lakin, M., *Interpersonal Encounter,* New York: McGraw-Hill, 1972.

Lifton, Walter M., *Working with Groups,* New York: Wiley, 1961.

Lingwood, David Alfred, *Interpersonal Communication,* Ann Arbor, Mich.: University Microfilm, 1970.

Luft, Joseph, *Group Processes,* Palo Alto, Calif.: National Press, 1963.

Luft, Joseph, *Of Human Interaction,* Palo Alto, Calif.: National Press, 1971.

Mann, Richard D., in collaboration with Graham S. Gibbard and John J. Hartman, *Interpersonal Style and Group Development,* New York: Wiley, 1967.

Markham, James W., *International Communication as a Field of Study,* Iowa City, Iowa: International Communication Division, Association for Education in Journalism, 1970.

Matson, Floyd and Ashley Montagu, *The Human Dialogue,* New York: Free Press, 1967.

McCroskey, James C., Carl E. Larson and Mark L. Knapp, *An Introduction to Interpersonal Communication,* Englewood Cliffs, N.J.: Prentice-Hall, 1971.

McLuhan, Marshall and Quentin Fiore, *The Medium is the Message,* New York: Random House, 1967.

Mehrabian, Albert, *Non-Verbal Communication,* Chicago: Aldine Publications, 1972.

Mehrabian, Albert, *Silent Messages,* Belmont Calif.: Wadsworth, 1967.

Merton, Robert K., *Social Theory and Social Structure,* New York: Free Press, 1957.

Miller, George A., *Communication and Language,* New York: Basic Books, 1967.

Mortensen, C. David, *Communication,* New York: McGraw-Hill, 1972.

Olmsted, Michael S., *The Small Group,* New York: Random House, 1959.

Parry, John, *Psychology of Human Communication,* New York: American Elsevier, 1968.

Phillips, Gerald M., *Communication and the Small Group,* Indianapolis: Bobbs-Merrill, 1966.

Phillips, Gerald M. and Eugene C. Erikson, *Interpersonal Dynamics in the Small Group,* New York: Random House, 1970.

Richardson, Lee, *Dimensions of Communication,* New York: Appleton-Century-Crofts, 1969.

Rogers, Everett M., *Communication of Innovations,* New York: Free Press, 1971.

Rosenberg, B. and D. M. White, *Mass Culture Revisited,* New York: Van Nostrand-Reinhold, Co., 1971.

Roslansky, John D., *Communication,* New York: Fleet Press, 1969.

Ruesch, Jurgen and Gregory Bateson, *Communication: The Social Matrix of Psychiatry,* New York: W. W. Norton, 1951, 1968.

Ruesch, Jurgen, *Disturbed Communication,* New York: Norton, 1957.

Reusch, Jurgen and Weldon Kees, *Nonverbal Communication,* Berkeley, Calif.: University of California Press, 1956, 1972.

Reusch, Jurgen, *Therapeutic Communication,* New York: Norton, 1961.

Schein, Edgar H. and Warren G. Bennis, *Personal and Organizational Change Through Group Methods,* New York: Wiley, 1965.

Schramm, Wilbur, *The Science of Human Communication,* New York: Basic Books, 1963.

Schroder, H. M., M. J. Driver and S. Streufer, *Human Information Processing,* New York: Holt, Rinehart and Winston, 1967.

Sereno, Kenneth K. and C. David Mortensen (eds.), *Foundations of Communication Theory,* New York: Harper, 1970.

Shands, Harley, *Thinking and Psychotherapy,* Cambridge, Mass.: Harvard University Press, 1960.

Shibutani, Tamotsu, *Society and Personality,* Englewood Cliffs, N.J.: Prentice-Hall, 1961.

Smith, Alfred G., *Communication and Culture,* New York: Holt, Rinehart and Winston, 1966.

Tepper, Albert and Paul Roman, *Oral Communication,* Minneapolis, Minnesota: Burgess Publishing, 1968.

Thayer, Lee, *Communication and Communication Systems,* Homewood, Ill.: Richard D. Irwin, 1968.

Tiger, Lionel, *Men in Groups,* New York: Random House, Vintage Books, 1969.

Tompkins, Charles, *Concepts of Communication,* New York: Wiley, 1971.

Vickers, Geoffrey, *Value Systems and Social Process,* New York: Basic Books, 1968.

Watzlawick, Paul, Janet H. Beavin and Don D. Jackson, *Pragmatics of Human Communication,* New York: W. W. Norton, 1967.

Weaver, Carl H., *Human Listening,* Indianapolis, Indiana: Bobbs-Merrill, 1972.

Whorf, B. L., *Language, Thought, and Reality,* Cambridge, Mass.: M.I.T. Press, 1956.

Wiener, N., *The Human Use of Human Beings,* New York: Avon, 1950.

Young, J. Z., *Doubt and Certainty in Science,* New York: Oxford University Press, 1950.

Part 3
COMMUNICATION SYSTEMS

Whether one chooses to focus attention on inter-group, community, societal, international, cross-cultural, or mass communication processes, each can be regarded as a communication system composed of inter-linkages between interacting and co-determining information processing subsystems. These subsystems, in turn, are composed of smaller subsubsystems, which may be composed of still smaller social units, the basic unit of which is the individual. As the number of parts—individuals, subsubsystems, and subsystems—within a system increase, the nature and complexity of the communication processes involved also increase at a dramatic rate. For each individual added to a network, there is an additional, potentially differing set of concepts, values, expectations, and knowledges which the subsystem, and ultimately the total system, must in some fashion accommodate. So it is, for example, with the community, where each new resident contributes to and must be accommodated at various levels by the community system. He affects and is affected by the neighborhood, colleagues in business, schools, churches, political and economic subsystems and, ultimately, the total community system.

It is through informational transactions in and with the larger encompassing system that the individual's orientation toward critical aspects of his world will be established, maintained and/or altered. At the same time, it is the collection of individuals together with their particular orientations which necessitate the development, maintenance and/or alteration in the larger encompassing system.

As noted previously, for each two or more person subsubsystem, there is a social organization achieved and maintained through social communication. Through social communication, knowledge, values, norms, standards, ethics, laws, rules, and roles are defined and information about them diffused to individuals who collectively compose the system. Through the mass media, and other mass communication institutions, each generation comes to learn much of the past, such that the child is not required (or allowed) to invent the world or its knowledge for himself.

There are, of course, intricate interrelationships between the individual, the personal communication processes, the social unit, and social communication. These interrelationships are critical to the nature and continuing viability of the larger, encompassing system, since the relationship between the individual and social unit may be mutually stabilizing, mutually divergent, or differentially impactful on particular subsystems within a larger system. Common to all communication systems is the characteristic of "interconnectedness"; change in one subsystem will foster change in the nature and/or function of other subsystems and of the system as a whole. Thus, a fuel shortage in Japan, for example, may have important consequences for economic operations not only in Japan, but in Western countries and, ultimately, for the world as a whole.

The simulations and games included in this section are designed to sharpen participant awareness of the complexity and interrelatedness of subsystems and their relationship to various systems which encompass them. Clearly, however, these generic phenomena cannot be duplicated in a single, or even in several classroom simulations. It is possible, though, to provide a dynamic context in which participants can gain a sense of these interrelationships in theory as well as in practice, while at the same time gaining a personal sense of the role they themselves play in these processes. The activities included in each exercise focus upon particular kinds of communication systems, ranging from inter-group to inter-cultural and mass communication. They are constructed to provide relatively low risk, time-compressed experiences in which participants can act and experience the consequences of their actions within a relatively complex, dynamic, and varigated human communication system.

Because the focus of these experiential techniques is upon the nature of communication systems, they are generally more complex and more demanding than other activities in this volume in terms of time requirements, extent of participant involvement, and requisite facilitator sophistication. For this reason it is recommended that these simulations and games be utilized only after a progression of more basic experience-based activities have been used, such as those presented in the sections of this volume dealing with personal and social communication. It is also recommended that some participants serve as observers during each simulation or game. For post-activity discussion and analysis, the perspective afforded by a detached observer-participant will be most useful. It will also be necessary for the facilitator to familiarize him or herself as thoroughly as possible with the concepts of personal and social communication, the literature on experience-based learning, and the material on communication systems suggested in the bibliographic portions of this book to ensure optimum utilization of these simulations and games.

36. Intergroup Organization

The exercise focuses upon intragroup cooperation and intergroup competition, group planning and decision making, and aspects of organizations and control. Allow between 45 and 90 minutes to complete the operational portion of the exercise, and an additional 20 to 30 minutes for discussion. The exercise may be used with almost any size group; a minimum of three groups of six to eight participants each is necessary.

Procedure:

1. Procure an ample supply of styrofoam locking blocks (Kenner or Romper Room are two such suppliers) so that each group will have 30 to 40 blocks of differing sizes to work with.
2. Prior to the exercise, the facilitators build a "master" model which each group will try to replicate (the more complicated the model, the greater the planning and organization needed to replicate it).
3. Divide the participants into groups of six to eight persons each. Each group should have its own table or floor space in which to work.
4. Give each group a few minutes to elect one of its members to serve on a "board of directors" which will be charged with supervising the activity.
5. Call the representatives of the groups to a central point in the room, and publicly give them the following instructions:
   a. The purpose of this exercise is to have each task group replicate this model (the "master" model should be placed on the table or stool in some central location).
   b. This group (the board) will *make* and *enforce* all rules by which the building shall proceed.
   c. Upon completion of the building, the board will select the winning group.
   d. The exercise is completed when the board informs the instructors that they have carried out *a, b,* and *c* above.
6. The master model and enough loose blocks to allow each group to complete the model are placed in control of the board of directors, and the instructors withdraw from all active participation in the exercise until step *d* above. (Facilitators will find it wise, for later discussion, not only to transmit the rules to the board verbally, but to write them—as stated—on a flip chart, as well.) During the exercise, instructors may serve as process observers.

Discussion:

The guidelines given by the instructors are intended to be ambiguous in order to provide the board of directors and the participants with maximum freedom to operate. With minimum constraints, the participants are limited only by their assumptions about "proper" behavior and social order. The most useful discussions following this exercise will focus on those issues. It is usually useful to begin the debriefing by facilitating discussion between the board and the participants, giving special attention to what the board intended by its rules and what the participants understood by them and how the rules affected participants' behavior. For example, if participants complain about the unfairness of the rules: If you objected to the rules, why didn't you raise questions prior to beginning building your model? Did your group obey rules it found unacceptable? What do you think the board was trying to accomplish by imposing such a rule? And for the board members: Did you anticipate the effects of such-and-such a rule? Did you consider asking participants to join in the rule-making? What did you intend for such-and-such a rule to accomplish? Were all board members agreed on all rules? Were any rules changed during the course of the exercise? If so, were all board members consulted before making exceptions? If not, why not?

Frequently a good deal of discussion will center on the methods for selecting a winning group. Facilitating questions for the judges may include: What criteria did you use for determining the winning group? How did you measure them? Were the criteria known in advance? If not, why not? For the participants: What did you understand as the meaning of such-and-such criterion? Did the criteria for winning govern your group's activity? If you did not know the criteria in advance, what assumptions was your group operating under?

Further questions can be formulated concerning each group's internal operations and leadership; their feelings of competitiveness with other groups; the degree of involvement by various group members; etc.

Variations:

Depending upon the instructor's goals, a number of variations may be introduced in this exercise.

1. In addition to selecting a member of the board, each group may wish also to select a team captain.
2. To further stress communication networks, a rule can be introduced that only team captains may talk with board members, and team captains then must relay board instructions to the group members.
3. The "master" model may be kept in a separate room, thus requiring heavier reliance upon verbal communication in completion of the task.
4. Purposely bias distribution of blocks so that no one group can complete the task without acquiring certain blocks from other groups, to underscore intergroup communication and cooperation.

37. Task Planning and Intergroup Coordination

This exercise is designed to focus on intra- and inter-group communication processes. The activity involves two groups, one of which has access to the information needed to complete the specified task. The other does not and must rely on the instructions they receive from the group which possesses the knowledge. The exercise can be used with 25 or fewer participants and requires one to two hours.

Materials:
    —14" × 14" piece of sturdy cardboard
    —4 envelopes

Procedure:
1. Using the detailed diagram provided in Fig. 37.1 as a ½ scale template, cut the pattern out of cardboard. (The four diagonal lines should be heavy black ones. The cross-hatch center portion is a hollow area.)

HOLLOW SQUARE PATTERN

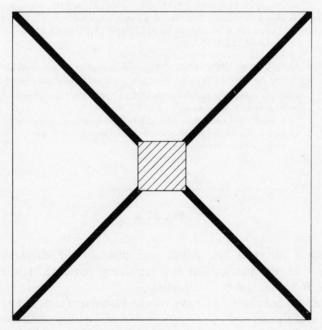

Fig. 37.1

HOLLOW SQUARE

BRIEFING FOR OBSERVING TEAM

You will be observing a situation in which a PLANNING TEAM decides how to solve a problem and gives instructions to an OPERATING TEAM for implementation. The problem consists of assembling 16 pieces of cardboard into the form of a hollow square. The PLANNING TEAM is supplied with the general layout of the pieces. This team is not to assemble the parts itself but is to instruct the OPERATING TEAM on how to assemble the parts in a minimum amount of time. You will be silent observers throughout the process.

Suggestions for Observation

1. Each member of the OBSERVING TEAM should watch the general pattern of communication but give special attention to one member of the PLANNING TEAM (during the planning phase) and one member of the OPERATING TEAM (during the assembling period).
2. During the Planning period watch for such behavior as this:
   a. The evenness or unevenness of participation among PLANNING TEAM members.
   b. Behavior that blocks or facilitates understanding.
   c. How the Planning Team divides its time between planning and instructing (how early does it invite the OPERATING TEAM to come in?).
   d. How well it plans its procedure for giving instructions to the OPERATING TEAM.
3. During the instructing period (when the PLANNING TEAM is instructing the OPERATING TEAM) watch for such things as these:
   a. Who in the PLANNING TEAM gives the instructions? How was this decided?
   b. How is the OPERATING TEAM oriented to the task?
   c. What assumptions made by the PLANNING TEAM are not communicated to the OPERATING TEAM?
   d. How full and clear were the instructions?
   e. How did the OPERATING TEAM members react to the instructions?
   f. Did the OPERATING TEAM feel free to ask questions of the planners?
4. During the assembly period (when the OPERATING TEAM is working alone) watch for such things as these:
   a. Evidence that instructions were clearly understood or misunderstood.
   b. Non-verbal reactions of PLANNING TEAM members as they watch their plans being implemented or distorted.

Fig. 37.2

2. Place 4 pieces of the puzzle into three of the envelopes and 5 pieces of the puzzle into the remaining envelope, labeling them B-1, B-2, B-3, and B-4, respectively.
3. Choose 4 individuals to serve on the Planning Team and send them out of the room.
4. Choose 4 other individuals for the Operating Team and send them to another room where they can be comfortable for a period.

5. Distribute Briefing Sheets and Observers Notes for the Observing Team (as provided in Figs. 37.2 and 37.3) to all individuals not assigned to either team. Provide the observers time to read and study their instructions. Emphasize that the observers are to gather closely around the Planning Team once assembled, and to be ready to lead discussion after the exercise has been completed.

6. Gather the Planning Team around a Table in the center of the room. Place the 4 envelopes on a table. Give the Planning Team one copy each of (a) Planning Team Briefing Sheet provided in Fig. 37.4 (b) Hollow Square Pattern provided in Fig. 37.1 and (c) Assembled Pattern provided in Fig. 37.5.

7. Instruct the group that all necessary instructions are on their Briefing Sheet. Answer any questions with the phrase, "All you need to know is on the Briefing Sheet."

HOLLOW SQUARE

OBSERVER'S NOTES

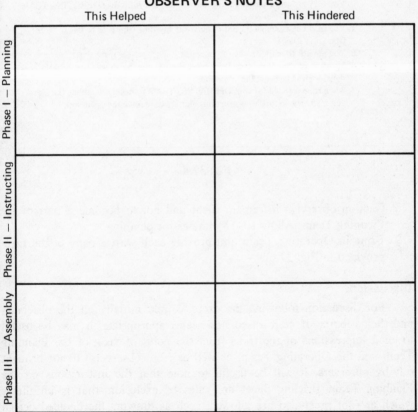

	This Helped	This Hindered
Phase I — Planning		
Phase II — Instructing		
Phase III — Assembly		

Fig. 37.3

HOLLOW SQUARE

BRIEFING SHEET FOR PLANNING TEAM

Each of you will be given a packet containing _____ cardboard pieces which, when properly assembled, will make a hollow square design.

Your Task

During a period of _____ minutes you are to do the following:
1. Plan how the 17 pieces distributed among you should be assembled to make the design.
2. Instruct your OPERATING TEAM on how to implement your plan (you may begin instructing your OPERATING TEAM at any time during the planning period — but <u>no later than</u> 5 minutes before they are to begin the assembling process).

General Rules

1. You must keep all pieces you have in front of you at all times.
2. You may <u>not</u> touch or trade pieces with other members of your team during the planning or instructing phase.
3. You may <u>not</u> show the sheet with the detailed design to the OPERATING TEAM at any time.
4. You may <u>not</u> assemble the entire square at any time (this is to be left to your Operating Team).
5. You are <u>not</u> to mark on any of the pieces.
6. Members of your Operating Team must also observe the above rules until the signal is given to begin the assembling.
7. When time is called for your OPERATING TEAM to begin assembling the pieces you may give no further instructions, but are to observe the operation.

Fig. 37.4

8. Caution observers to remain silent and not to become a part of the Planning Team. Allow 10–15 minutes for planning.
9. Bring in Operating Team and provide each with a copy of the form provided in Fig. 37.6.

Discussion:

For discussion following the exercise, rely initially on the observers and their reports. If more discussion seems appropriate, it may be useful to elicit impressions of the tasks from the point of view of the Planning Team and the Operating Team, as well as from observers. If not brought out by observers, it will be useful to note that the instructions on the Planning Team Briefing Sheet are rules of exclusion—that is all things which are not precluded are allowed, such as drawing the detailed design on the Hollow Square Pattern, drawing a template on the table, on another sheet of paper, numbering the pieces of the puzzle, etc. Usually

ASSEMBLED PATTERN

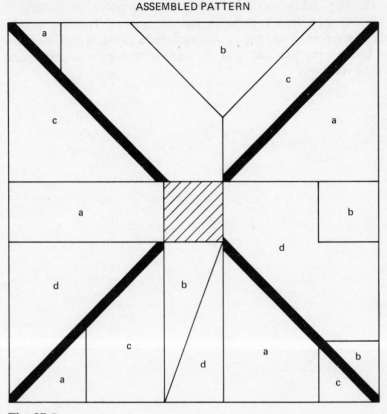

Fig. 37.5

Fig. 37.6

1. You will have responsibility for carrying out a task for 4 people according to instructions given by your PLANNING TEAM. Your PLANNING TEAM may call you in for instructions at any time. If they do not summon you before _____ you are to report to them anyway. Your task is scheduled to begin promptly at _____ , after which no further instructions from your PLANNING TEAM can be given. You are to finish the assigned task as rapidly as possible.

2. During the period when you are waiting for a call from your PLANNING TEAM it is suggested that you discuss and make notes on the following:
   a. The feelings and concerns which you experience while waiting for instructions for the unknown task.
   b. Your suggestions on how a person might prepare to receive instructions.

3. The notes recorded on the above will be helpful during the work group discussions following the completion of your task.

the Planning Team makes a variety of assumptions about their roles which keep them from considering such alternatives. This then leads to a useful discussion of the role of assumptions in planning and the relationship between the processes and problems of this exercise and others in differing contexts.

38. Conflict, Confrontation, and Conflict Resolution

This exercise is designed to increase understandings of the processes of conflict, confrontation, and conflict resolution as they relate to individuals and groups trying to complete a task. The activity requires several hours and can be used appropriately with groups of 8 to 25 participants.

Materials:

—large sheets of heavy construction paper, cut into puzzle pieces forming two separate and distinct puzzles, plus a number of "Filler" pieces which fit no puzzle.
—Box with slot cut in top.
—Roll of crepe paper
—prizes for winners

Procedure:

1. Divide the total group of participants into two sub-groups or teams according to height or eye color. One group, "The Talls" or "The Blue Eyes" have a number of advantages as they compete with the other group to complete a puzzle.

2. Inform both groups that they are to compete to assemble a puzzle (a different one is provided for each team) in the shortest length of time. There are prizes for the winners.

3. The use of ashtrays, waste baskets, door, and so on can be granted only by the group with special jurisdiction (e.g., "The Talls"). Jurisdiction over all cigarettes and matches, as well as such items as gum and candy may also be granted by the instructor to the advantaged team.

4. To gain access to any of the items listed, or to gain a privilege or service, the requesting group must render some service or make some concession—that is, earn the service, object or privilege. Just what the service or concession should be, is determined through mutual bargaining. Any agreement must be approved by the majority of both teams.

5. The group requesting some item or privilege can send only one person at a time to *officially* represent their interests to the other group. This however does not preclude talking, calling, or any other form of communication within or between teams.

6. Each team is informed that their goal is the completion of their puzzle and instructed that each team will have an undisclosed number of puzzle pieces to assemble. (Though nothing will be said overtly, each team will have pieces from two puzzles and some "filler" pieces that go to nothing.) Also in the middle of the room there will be a "transaction table" where there will be a box con-

taining some more pieces from the two puzzles together with some "filler" pieces. The positioning of the transaction table and the layout of the room are presented in Fig. 38.1.

7. Should a group in attempting to complete its puzzle, find that they do not possess all of the pieces they need, they then have one of two sources for the needed pieces: 1) the transaction table box, and 2) the other team. The privilege of going to the puzzle box and withdrawing a piece (one at a time), SIGHT UNSEEN, can only be granted by the opposing team in the following manner: The side requesting to go to the puzzle piece box on the transaction table must send one member of their group, who is selected by the other team, to a public questioning, conducted by the opposing team in their territory. The questioning group devises three questions for the person. He must answer at least one of the three correctly for them to grant him the privilege of withdrawing a puzzle piece. If a team whose representative fails to answer any of the three questions correctly or has any complaint or protest (concerning the type of question, judgment of answers, etc.), it may send three members to discuss the complaint with three members of the other side. A simple majority ruling (4 out of 6) is sufficient for settlement.

8. Should either side wish to acquire puzzle pieces or other objects or services from the other, the requesting group should render some

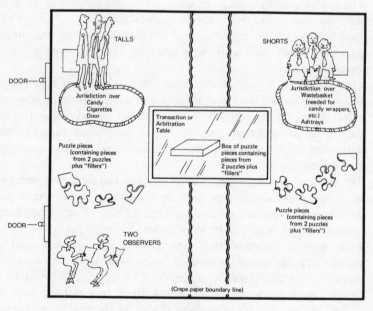

Fig. 38.1

service, make some concession, or earn them in some way, the criteria of which shall be determined by the other team. In no case is direct trading of pieces permitted.

9. Before actually beginning the exercise select two observers (minimum) whose job it will be to observe, report upon and lead discussion on the exercise following its completion.

10. At a point in time when conflict seems to be moving toward a high, the exercise is called to a halt.

11. The symbolic boundary line between teams is removed and the instructor informs both groups that: "You are now on your own. All former restrictions are off and you are to do things your own way; we're throwing the rules open to you and you can resolve the matter in any way you like!"

12. After an appropriate period of time, perhaps after one or both puzzles have been completed stop the activity and ask observers to lead the entire group in a discussion.

Discussion:

A number of catalysts are built into this exercise to promote conflict and confrontation. Among them are jurisdictional privileges over the physical facilities including access to the door, lights, etc. The physical division into two groups in a manner which suggests that one is better than the other, as with Talls vs. Shorts provides an additional component of agitation. Mixing of the puzzle pieces such that each group must of necessity deal with the other and the center box of pieces over which both groups share control also fosters critical interactions. The mechanisms for questioning of participants by the other team provide for confrontation and leave wide open the nature and extent of conflict which may arise as a consequence. During discussion these issues may well be identified as critical factors in determining the nature and direction of activity. If they are not brought out by the observers or participants, the instructor may wish to be certain they are considered. Did conflict occur? Why? What factors seemed crucial to its development? Was frustration felt by participants of either or both groups? How was it manifested? How was it resolved? Were interactions between groups functional? Did a high sense of competition between teams develop? Was there more or less participation by all members of both groups? Why or why not? What thoughts and feelings remain even after the exercise has ended? How do aspects of the frustration, conflict, confrontation, and conflict resolution, which may have occured in this activity, compare to real life occurrences?

39. Mass Communication and Community Decision-Making

The following game focuses on the complex range of interests and opinions which exist within a community around an issue that is crucial to the future of the area. It also emphasizes the role of mass communication in observing, reporting, gathering, categorizing and packaging information reflecting the various perspectives of relevance in the community.

The game involves a hypothetical corporation—NRG, which deals in power and utilities. The firm wishes to build a nuclear power plant outside of Midtown, a moderate-size New England community. Midtown was a one-industry textile town during the nineteenth and first half of the twentieth century. During the 1950s the textile company moved its plant to North Carolina. Since then, Midtown has been trying to attract other industries to support their depressed economy.

The nuclear plant cannot be built without authorization through a referendum. As the time for the referendum approaches, the various factions in Midtown mount their campaigns to persuade the voters to pass or defeat the measure. In such an instance, the flow of information is crucial to the outcome. The purpose of this simulation is to enable the participants to experience and examine the interplay that affects this flow of information, and provide them with a more sophisticated approach to obtaining and processing all information received through media.

Procedure:

1. Each participant receives a card casting him in a role with a specific objective to fulfill within the simulation.
2. The end product of the simulation maybe a newspaper, magazine, or speech, produced by those cast in mass communication roles, as a result of their interviews and research with the other characters in the community.

Discussion:

Discussion can be focused both on the final mass communication product, and upon the process involved in gathering, ordering, sorting, categorizing and interpreting the events which are presented in the final report.

Character Cards:

Publisher—You are the publisher of the only mass medium in Midtown. Naturally, the economy of the town affects the livelihood of your enterprise. The new tax money that the nuclear plant will provide, the jobs it will create, and the business it will generate will add to your advertising and circulation revenue. *You would like to see the nuclear plant built.*

Editor/Manager — You are the managing editor of the only mass medium in Midtown and have been so for twenty years. *Your object is to see that your medium researches every facet* of the proposed plant so that the voters have adequate information on which to base their decision.

Editorial Manager —You are the manager of the editorial comment of the only medium in Midtown. You feel that the known and unknown by-products and waste from nuclear plants present ecological and health hazards that outweigh the economic values of locating the industry near the town. *Your objective is to persuade the voters,* through your communications, to defeat the referendum.

President, Midtown Chamber of Commerce —For over a decade, Midtown has been seriously depressed, financially. As President of the Chamber of Commerce, you can see an economic boom resulting from the building of the nuclear plant. *Your objective is to persuade your fellow citizens to support the referendum.*

President, Board of Education — It has been difficult to maintain and run the Midtown school system with the cuts in budget necessitated by the financial straits of the town. The nuclear plant will contribute enormous new tax monies that will relieve the situation and enable modernization of school, curriculum and staff. This influx of money would greatly ease your problems, so the prospect of building the plant strikes you favorably. *Your objective is to use your influence as conscience dictates* as the investigation proceeds.

Chairman, City Council of Midtown —The lack of money and the resulting inertia has made your role as Chairman of the City Council a difficult one. *Your objective is to see the nuclear plant built* so that the resulting prosperity will create a favorable climate for your re-election.

Reporter —You are a reporter for the only mass medium in Midtown. The managing editor assigns you to do an investigative series on the building of the nuclear plant and its possible effects on the town. You are an ardent conservationist and have been working in mass communication since graduation from college four years ago. *Your objective is to dig up as many facts and figures* as possible to give the voters an opportunity to exercise their franchise intelligently.

Copyreader/Supervisor — You are a copyreader for the only mass communication vehicle in Midtown. In your checks and balance role, you edit the reporter's copy, checking facts, style, grammar and bias. *Your objective is to be sure the young reporter's personal convictions don't distort the series on the nuclear plant.*

President, NRG —As President of NRG, you are most anxious to have the nuclear plant built at Midtown, for there has been increasing opposition to the development of nuclear plants in every area of the country. *Your objective is to emphasize the financial gains* to the Midtown community, concealing or minimizing, as much as possible, the potential hazards from nuclear waste.

Local Chairman, Conservation Society – Your group is opposed to the construction of the nuclear plant on the grounds that the nuclear waste will pollute the soil and water. *Your objective is to offer enough documentation that will persuade the voters to defeat the referendum.*

40. Communication and Intra-Community Problem-Solving

Superhighway is a simulation game that is designed to underscore the dependence of members of communities upon one another for their mutual existence. It is also intended to demonstrate the nature of communication processes within such a community system. The activity can be used with 15 to 35 participants and requires approximately one and one-half hours.

The problem facing the participants in this exercise—the residents of Simsburg—is a proposed superhighway, U.S. 135, which if approved, would connect Bradburg and Carson, bypassing Simsburg.

Materials needed for this simulation game consist of role descriptions, map of hypothetical area, decision cards and final result cards. The content of each is presented on the following pages.

Procedure:

1. Participants are asked to select one of the following occupational roles in numbers which roughly correspond to:

1 mayor	3 teachers
1 religious leader	4 filling station owners
1 diner owner	5 large city manufacturers
1 radical townsman	4 housewives
3 truck drivers	6 factory workers

2. The map of the area, provided in Fig. 40.1, is displayed and the legend explained, pointing out and discussing the proposed superhighway route.
3. Role descriptions are distributed to participants who read and carefully study their roles, preparing themselves to play the part of the person described.
4. Participants assigned identical roles are provided time (five to ten minutes) to interact with one another to discuss the relative merits of the two proposed superhighway routes.
5. A town meeting is called by the mayor. Each participant will be asked by the mayor to offer a proposal, make comments and offer suggestions regarding the situation in the community; from the viewpoint of the role character he has assumed.
6. Decision cards are made available for distribution. Each participant should carefully consider all possible alternatives in light of the discussion at the town meeting. (A participant may choose a course of action different from those proposed at the town meeting.)
7. Each participant selects the decision card closest to the decision he has elected.

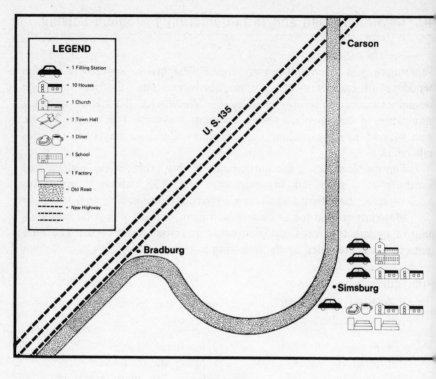

Fig. 40.1

8. Final result cards are distributed. Each participant must select the card with the letter corresponding to that on his decision card.

Discussion:

Were the final outcomes surprising? Were they logical? Did participants find difficulty maintaining the attitudes and values prescribed by the assigned roles? Did the roles seem realistic? Was the community problem a realistic one? Was the simulation game realistic? In what ways? Were the final outcomes realistic? What values are implied? How effective was communication among different community members? Discuss. Desribe the communication processes that occurred during the two meetings. If the game were repeated, would participants select the same role? Why? Why not? Other than highways, are there parallels between this situation and others in society?

Character Cards

Diner owner I am 30 years old and was raised in the restaurant business. I get some business from the town but like the filling stations, my diner depends on either truckers or travelers for most of its customers.

I am very upset about the building of the new highway but haven't as yet decided what to do. I could keep my business but I would have to lower my standard of living, or I could move to a big city and look for a job working in someone else's diner. I have no family to worry about but hate to leave.

Truck Driver I am in my middle 30's. I am married and the father of 3 children. I was born in this town and have worked as a truck driver for the past 18 years. The pay scale of my job is adequate, but I would like to be able to provide my family with more of the better things in life. With the building of the new highway, I have been offered a big raise in pay. I realize what the new highway will do to the town, but I must also think of my family. With my increased salary, my family and I will be able to afford to move to the big city.

Religious Leader Brethren, I am 63 years old and have been with you and watched you and your children grow and multiply. I have seen many changes over the years, all of which our town has survived. You may feel that this highway is a big threat to our town, but I know that if we stand united this obstacle like all the others will be overcome. We must not lose sight of our spiritual strength for in the end that will be the factor enabling us to win this battle. I am sure that the highway department will reconsider their proposal. We must remain united and wait.

Filling-Station Owner I am one of four filling-station owners in this town. In the past there has always been enough business for all of us. When completed, this highway will cause business to drop to practically nothing and leave us with no financial alternative but to move to the city. I have more to lose than any of you since I have no other skills. The decision I have made is the only practical choice for any of us.

Teacher I am 27 years old and unmarried. I grew up in this town and was educated in Carson. Deciding to share my education with my home town, I returned in order to teach here. I am much concerned with the present problem. However, schools in the large cities do have much to offer if you decide to move. It will be as difficult for me to leave Simsburg as it will be for you, but I feel that we may all profit in the end.

City Manufacturer I am 45 years old. I am a self-made man. I have found through the years that success comes only through self-interest and hard work. Because of the present non-direct route of delivery I have lost thousands of dollars. The new highway will help me compensate for my losses. The new route is much faster, more economical, and therefore the practical solution to my problem.

You townspeople must realize that you are in no position to fight the power of "big business." If you could see the problem as I do you would realize that the decision has already been made.

Factory Worker I am 50 years old and have been working in the factory for 30 years. Should it close, moving to a new community would be next to impossible for me. Not many employers will hire persons my age. A family of seven is a great financial burden and I cannot put myself in a position where my livelihood is jeopardized. My home is paid for and we live comfortably. I cannot be sure that a move could give me as much security. The new highway is a threat to us all. We must try to save our town.

Housewife I am 43 years old and the mother of five children. My husband and I came to this town 18 years ago. We like it here. We have established a home and made many close friends. Our church group has done a great deal to better our community. Since my children are of school age, I feel that a move would be too much of an adjustment for them. Financially, we are in no position to make such a move anyway.

I propose that the Women's League unite and form a picket line along the highway in order to appeal to travelers. In this way maybe, we can make our voices heard. I just do not know where else to turn for help.

Mayor I am 55 years old and your elected representative. I am well aware of your feelings concerning the present problem.

Since we cannot stop the highway from being built we must consider other possible measures. I propose that we petition the Highway Commission to have a bypass built through our town. In this way, we will be connected with the new highway. However, I must be aboveboard with you and tell you that this process could be a slow one. In the event that our petition is rejected, many of us will be left with only one alternative that is, to yield to the Federal Highway Commission and leave our town. I hope that you will consider my proposal and not discard it without careful consideration.

Radical Townsman I am 24 years old and single. I was born and raised in this town and many of my family and relatives still live here. I attended college in Carson and have developed a bad attitude toward city people. Their only concern is money. They would just as soon destroy this small town as see it grow. They care nothing about us, therefore we must care about ourselves.

Of course, we could stand and wait as our spiritual leader suggests or we could just pack up and leave as some small business owners suggest. Our Mayor suggests the alternative of petitioning the Highway Commission—but do you realize that the process takes, at the very least, 6 years.

We have been unable to reason with these people, because they consider us inferior. They leave us no choice other than to fight back. Let us rise up and show them that we too can take action. I propose that 2 weeks from this very day we bomb the highway!

41. Society, Communication and Power

This game is almost totally unstructured, and depends entirely upon the actions and interactions of the players for direction. It focuses upon the nature of the communication between diverse individuals within society (in this case a game society), each with differing goals and, often, with unique ways of interacting with each other in pursuit of those goals.

The activity can be played by groups of 5 to 12 participants, and requires from 1 to 5 hours to play.

Procedure:

1. Materials required include a number of four-inch-square pieces of colored poster board. Use approximately 10 squares for each participant. One-third of the squares should be one color, one-third another color, and one-third of still another color. In addition, a large quantity of one-inch squares of poster board of the same colors as the larger squares are needed (allow roughly 30 per participant). Several pairs of scissors, ample colored pencils, pens or magic markers, and a die are required.

2. Thoroughly shuffle the four-inch squares and lay them out on the floor or table so as to form a large, square gameboard. The board will be composed of roughly equal numbers of squares of the three colors, randomly distributed. A game board for, say, ten players would be a large 10×10 square containing 100 four-inch square pieces.

3. Each player takes a quantity of one-inch squares, selecting only one color to be used by him throughout the game. Each player proceeds to make his own playing pieces from these one-inch squares. The pieces may take any form the player elects to construct using the pencils and scissors.

4. Each player, in turn, rolls the die to determine the number of pieces with which he begins the game.

5. The player who rolls the lowest number (and hence will have the fewest number of pieces) begins. On his first move he places anywhere on the board, the number of pieces corresponding to the number he rolled on the die.

6. The player who rolled the next to the lowest number begins his turn in the same manner, and so on through to the player who rolled the highest number. This sequence then establishes the order of play for the remainder of the game.

7. On the second round of play, and on every round thereafter, each player may add up to three new pieces to the board. After adding his pieces, he may move any or all other pieces on the board, in-

cluding those of other players. He may remove any pieces from the board he wishes, or destroy any pieces he wishes. He must however, engage in these activities only during his turn of play.

8. In the event that any player finds that all of his pieces have been removed or destroyed, he may, on his next turn, re-enter the game by placing up to three new pieces on the board.

9. It should be made clear at the beginning of the game that each players's pieces, moves and strategies have a significance known only to him. About all of the other pieces on the board he knows only three things: they are mobile, they are vulnerable, and they are significant. He may, of course, talk with any other player he wishes during the course of the game.

10. Play continues until all players agree that the game is ended. Participants may drop out of the game at any time by removing their pieces and announcing their withdrawal.

Discussion:

This game will generate its own discussion, particularly if play has been long and intense. Players will seek to question other players about their goals, strategies, moves, and reaction to those of other players. The strength of the exercise lies in the fact that it is a highly personal game, reflecting each individual's competitiveness, cooperativeness, persistence, ingenuity, ability to cope, and a host of other feelings and behaviors developed through his interactions with other players. The exercise serves as a catalytic agent, facilitating a wide range of interpersonal interchanges as well as personal introspection and self awareness.

42. Cross Cultural Communication: Introductions and Departures

This activity is designed to heighten awareness of how North American patterns of greeting and leave-taking differ from those in other parts of the world, and to increase awareness of one's own comfort level with touching and being touched. The activity is appropriately used with groups up to 40 participants and requires approximately 15 minutes for completion.

Procedure:

1. Divide the group into two subgroups, A and B. If possible the teams or groups should be visually distinguishable from one another. Colored ribbons, nametags, or armbands, are suitable.
2. Ask Team B to leave the room.
3. Instruct Team A members that when Team B comes back in the room they are to meet and greet their friends and business associates who are Team B members. Inform Team A members that they come from a culture where close contact and warm embraces are the traditional style of saying "hello." Point out that when they shake hands on encountering Team B members to prolong the hand-shake for at least 30 seconds. Then they should talk for a few minutes about how they are feeling. When the bell rings Team A members are to say "goodbye" by giving their partner a warm embrace.
4. Instruct Team B members that when they reenter the room they are to meet and greet members of Team A as friends and associates in the traditional North American fashion. They are to talk for a few minutes about how they are feeling, and when the bell rings, say "goodbye" using typical farewell gestures.
5. Following the completion of the exercise re-group both teams for discussion.

Discussion:

It has been often said that the English and their North American counterparts are impoverished when it comes to kinesic communication, that we tend to use words to denote what gesture or tone would express in other cultures. Do our greeting and farewell patterns really connote our true feelings? How did Team A feel when greeted by members of Team B? How did Team B feel? Were there different reactions at fare-well? Why? Why not? What factors contributed to comfortable feelings? What factors led to discomfort? Does age, sex, social status and rela-tionship determine in part how we say hello and goodbye? Do we greet males differently than females? Children differently than adults? Relatives the same as friends?

In North America we are quite reserved when greeting others. Body contact particularly between males is frowned upon, and holding hands is considered a sign of homosexual tendency. Yet in Arab countries men kiss each other on the street when they meet. Nigerian men often walk hand in hand, and Italian men embrace warmly and remain touching when engaged in conversation. In some African countries handshakes may be extended for long periods of time, and a hand on the knee among males is not an offense. How would you react to such signs of affection?

43. Cross Cultural Awareness and Stereotyping

This role playing exercise is designed to heighten awareness of gross cultural differences as barriers to communication. It can best be utilized with groups ranging from 15 to 45 and requires several hours to several days depending upon goals selected.

Procedure:

1. Divide the group into three subgroups.
2. Each group is assigned a particular cultural identity: either as a member of the country of *Agitania, Meditania* or *Solidania*.
3. Provide participants of each role with the character descriptions presented in Figs. 43.1 through 43.3, and ask that participants work at thinking and acting the way the cultural and behavioral models suggest.
4. Present the groups with a decision-making task in which they work together to arrive at a particular conclusion while operating as if they were Agitanians, Meditanians, and Solidanians, respectively. If time permits, it will be possible to allow participants acting in their roles, to interact normally over several days, without utilizing a specific exercise of decision-making.
5. Follow the period of role enactment with discussion.

CONFIDENTIAL:
TO BE SEEN BY AGITANIANS ONLY

Behavioral Characteristics of the Country of Agitania:

1. TACTILE: touch as much as possible, stand and sit close to people, and give a long hand-shake (about 15 seconds) when you greet a person.

2. EXTENSIVE EYE CONTACT: look a person in the eyes when you talk extensively to him.

3. SELF-ORIENTED: act selfishly. Talk about yourself and things that only interest you. You do not pay attention to the person you're talking to because he's not as important as you are to yourself and, therefore, you don't want to understand him better. You feel you're always right and the other person is wrong. You always interrupt people.

4. PHILOSOPHY OF CONFLICT: you like to argue for the sake of arguing so that people will pay attention to you.

5. NON-COOPERATIVE: you avoid helping people under any circumstances.

Fig. 43.1

CONFIDENTIAL:

TO BE SEEN BY MEDITANIANS ONLY

Behavioral Characteristics of the Country of Meditania:

1. SEMI-TACTILE: touch people only occasionally when you're talking. Stand and sit about an arm's length from a person. Give a short handshake when you're greeting a person.
2. MEDIUM EYE-CONTACT: look at a person in the eyes for only about 3 seconds at a time.
3. SHARING: when you're talking or doing things with a person, share <u>your</u> interests with him and let him share <u>his</u> interests with you. <u>Exchange</u> ideas. Talk <u>with</u> him instead of <u>to</u> him.
4. PHILOSOPHY OF RATIONALITY: when you're arguing or discussing something with a person, <u>listen first</u> to what he's saying, <u>then</u> say what you want to say, and <u>finally</u>, weigh in your mind the two different points of view before making a decision. Do <u>not</u> assume that he's wrong and you're right. Accept the fact that you <u>may be</u> wrong <u>sometimes</u> OR that you and he think differently.
5. SELF-INTEREST CO-OPERATION: you help another person <u>only</u> if it benefits you.

Fig. 43.2

CONFIDENTIAL:

TO BE SEEN BY SOLIDANIANS ONLY

Behavioral Characteristics of the Country of Solidania:

1. NON-TACTILE: do not touch, stand or sit close to other people; give no handshake (simply nod your head in greeting a person).
2. OTHER-PERSON-ORIENTED: you are inquisitive; get to know the other person by asking him questions about what he's interested in <u>instead</u> of talking about yourself. <u>Never</u> interrupt. Listen carefully and let a person finish what he is saying before you speak.
3. PHILOSOPHY OF ACCEPTANCE AND NON-VIOLENCE: never argue about a point with which you disagree. You want to avoid conflict situations.
4. MINIMAL EYE-CONTACT: avoid looking at a person in the eyes. If you happen to look at a person in the eyes, look for only a split second.
5. COOPERATIVE: you try to help other people (especially in solving a problem) as much as possible.

Fig. 43.3

Discussion:

The cultural/national roles participants are asked to assume in this exercise are, of course, not intended to be real. Rather the focus of the exercise is upon heightening awareness that there are in fact, cultural differences, which manifest themselves in communication behavior. Clearly, also there is no single cultural prototype, and to assume that one role description is adequate characterization of an entire culture would be to miss the opportunity to focus discussion upon the process of stereotyping itself.

Beyond this discussion, it will be useful for participants to share reactions to their roles, and any difficulties they may have encountered enacting them. What sorts of barriers came about between groups? Why? To what extent can a cultural description be accurate? In what ways do cultural differences of the sort exemplified by the roles lead to barriers in communication? What application does this activity have for everyday communication experiences?

44. Time, Timing, and Culture

This exercise is intended as a means of focusing upon the differences in time and timing in different cultures. It can be used usefully with groups up to 35 or 40 and requires approximately 15 minutes for completion.

Procedure:

1. Divide the group into two subgroups, A and B. If possible the teams or groups should be visually distinguishable from one another. Colored ribbons, nametags, or armbands, are suitable.
2. Ask Team B to leave the room.
3. Inform Team A that their group and the members of group B have an appointment with a photographer at 12:00 sharp to have pictures taken. Advise them that Team B is also aware of the time and place. Inform Team A that they are to behave as if they know that the photographer has another appointment at 12:30 in another part of town, and that they come from a culture where promptness is a virtue.
4. Instruct Team B that along with Team A they have an appointment to have a group picture taken in the large room at 12:00 sharp. Inform them that they come from a culture where time does not count. Take it easy, have a coffee . . . why rush!
5. Allow an appropriate amount of time to pass to enable a regrouping to occur for the hypothetical group photo.
6. After regrouping has been completed, move to discussion.

Discussion:

It has often been said that individuals in industrialized societies are "slaves to time." What happens to people who get in the way when there is a job to be done? Is following the clock the "right" way to organize one's life necessarily. How do we react to individuals in other cultures who take it easy, find time to laugh and play during "working" hours or who mix work and play?

How did Team A react to the members of Team B who exhibited so little concern for promptness. Was some active behavior more acceptable than others? What suggestions would you offer for resolving this sort of cultural and communication barrier to interpersonal relations. In many countries of the world and among some native peoples and ethnic groups in North America, a meeting called for noon may not actually begin until three o'clock. Can we learn to work with others whose conceptions of time differ from our own?

45. Communication and Development
Hypothetica: A Social Action Game

Hypothetica is designed to provide a context for fostering the simultaneous development of a variety of communication experiences and problems, and permits the unimpeded evolution of participant behavior for coping with that developing process. It was initially designed for and used extensively in international seminars as a game to deal with cross-cultural communication, development, change, and social organization and planning. While some of these dimensions will be missing when used in an American setting, it nonetheless remains an involving communication exercise focusing upon interpersonal, small group and community decision-making, the processes of conflict and resolution, the invention of strategies for influence and persuasion, the issues of leadership and power, and the planning and consequences of development and change.

Hypothetica can be played with as few as 12 and as many as 60 participants; the optimum number of players is 30. Depending upon the instructional objectives for employing the game, it can be played for as few as 90 minutes to as many as five days. Highly complex versions of the exercise have been developed so as to cover the course work of an entire semester.

Procedure:

1. Each participant receives a map of *Hypothetica* (Fig. 45.1) and a copy of the "National Characteristics and Problem" sheet. To establish the setting and focus of the exercise, the instructor reads through the sheet, informing participants they will receive more detailed information as the exercise proceeds. For both the presentation of the problem and later discussion, the instructor and participants will find a large reproduction of the map quite useful (an enlarged drawing on a flip chart works well). [The original version of this exercise includes 80 color slides of *Hypothetica's* countryside and people, and a 3 × 4 foot map of the country for use throughout the game.]

2. Following the introduction, participants are divided into five groups equal in size, representing the five districts of *Hypothetica*. The best physical arrangement for this segment of the exercise consists of five large tables well separated throughout the room. Whatever can be done by the instructor at this juncture to assist in building district identity will prove useful (e.g., providing signs or placards for each table displaying the district name—Southern, Central, etc.). Each member of each district caucus now receives a copy of the fact sheet appropriate to his region.

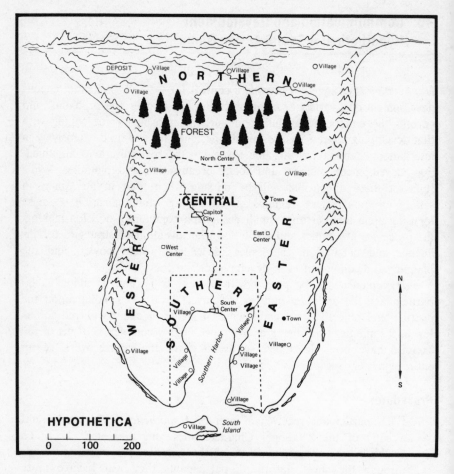

Fig. 45.1

3. Each delegation is instructed to elect a chairman and a vice-chairman, both to conduct the district discussions and to later represent the district at the "national conference" with *Hypothetica's* prime minister. Each district chairman is then given a complete set of fact sheets pertaining to the other four districts. (A variation of this procedure sometimes used to increase inter-group communication withholds fact sheets pertaining to other districts. Information concerning regions other than one's own must then be obtained through interpersonal channels.)

4. Prior to commencing district discussions, the instructor has one other decision to make: Who shall serve as Prime Minister and how shall that decision be reached? There are several possibilities: a) If the game is being conducted over a relatively short time span, and if

the game goals are relatively few and sharply focused (e.g., inter-group cooperation and competition, or the consensus process, or techniques of persuasion, etc.), then the role and function is best filled by having the instructor or one of his assistants serve as prime minister; b) the instructor selects a participant whom he feels can productively conduct the "national conference" in a manner consistent with the goals of the exercise; c) if time is not a factor, and the game is being employed as a broader simulation to unearth a wider range of behaviors and strategies, a general election involving all or a portion of the participants can be conducted. In any case, once the prime minister is selected, he should be excluded from district discussions.

5. Once the selection of the prime minister has been determined, the instructor should again restate the problem or problems of the exercise and commence the discussions at the district level. The focus of these discussions is regional, i.e., What does this mean to our region, now and in the future? Based on this assessment, what will be our position at the "national conference?"

6. Again, depending upon the time parameters, these discussions should consume approximately one-half the time allotted to the total exercise. The longer the district sessions, the more group solidarity and identification will be allowed to develop, which, for certain learning goals, can be advantageous.

7. The next phase of the exercise is the calling of the prime minister's national conference. This conference is "attended" by one official voting delegate (usually the chairman) and one alternate from each district. The best physical arrangement for this session is one large table with six chairs (one for each delegate and one for the prime minister) for the principals of the meeting. The remainder of the participants can sit by delegations behind their respective representatives. Representatives are encouraged to confer with their delegations throughout the conference. The discussions will be facilitated by placing the large map of *Hypothetica* where it can be easily referenced by all participants during the discussion.

8. The national conference is ended when some resolution has been reached regarding the initial set of problems. In shorter versions of the exercise, the instructor may wish to impose a time limit—either by issue or for the entire conference.

Discussion:

After several iterations of this exercise, the instructor will discover both its potential for richness as well as a number of variations for exploiting that potential. Perhaps the most important consideration in using the exercise lies in focusing upon the problem areas that will form the core of the discussion sessions. Shorter versions of the exercise can be expedited by stating certain givens. For example, rather than posing the broader question, "What action should be taken in regard to the mineral deposit?" the problem might be narrowed to "The decision has been made to move the ore from the deposit area to the harbor by single trunk railroad. The prime minister would like advice concerning the route of that railroad." (Obvious related questions such as refining, acquisition of private lands, the fate of the abundant national forest once penetrated by railroad, etc., make interesting additional problems for longer versions of the game.) No attempt will be made here to enumerate all the possible approaches to playing *Hypothetica,* since they are virtually limitless. Debriefing sessions following the exercise will, of course, be guided by the goals and questions used to structure the game initially.

If *Hypothetica* is being employed as a basic exercise in change and development, there is an additional presentation which has proved most effective particularly with international participants from developing countries. Once the debriefing is completed, the instructor asks participants to project themselves 30–40 years into the future, and leads a focused discussion on what changes have been brought about in *Hypothetica* as a result of exploitation of the deposit. Examples include: What has happened to the pace of life in *Hypothetica?* The standard of living? The growth of villages and population centers? Societal values and norms? What have been the effects of industrialization? Of increased and improved transportation (one can now travel from the Northern District to the Southern District in less than a day)? How has the influx of foreigners influenced the culture? What has become of indigent industries (such as fishing in the South)? Has exploitation of the mineral deposit brought on exploitation of other natural resources (the large natural forest reserve)? What systemic problems has conversion from an agrarian country to an industrial country brought about (labor problems, pollution, education, etc.)? The instructor can find a number of examples of countries (including the U.S.) that have passed through the process here described, and draw parallels pertaining to problems attending development and change. One of the key issues growing out of *Hypothetica* is the interrelatedness of events and the ways in which people act upon those events. While the central problem may have been the exploitation of the mineral deposit, a decision to act upon that problem triggers a complex network of related effects, many of which participants fail to take into account when seeking ways to solve the more immediate question.

Hypothetica:
National Characteristics and Problems

Hypothetica is a relatively small developing country with an extensive history of independence with little previous foreign contact. All of these factors can be attributed more to geographical considerations than political intention. The country is surrounded by rugged and virtually impenetrable mountains except for a large natural harbor located in the Southern district of the country. *Hypothetica* has a fairly balanced economy and, for the size of its population, is generally self sustaining—although there has been a marked increase in imports (mainly machinery and petroleum) over the past twenty years. The country can be divided roughly into five economic sectors, coinciding for the most part with the countries five district states: agriculture in the Eastern district; herding in the Western district; fishing in the Southern district; hunting and logging of lumber in the Northern district, and an active urban center in the east central plains area forming the Central district. The Central district is the seat of the national government in Capitol City, the business and banking center, and serves as a collection and redistribution point for resources processed through some light industry located there.

The population of the country is heavily concentrated in the Central District (which contains nearly half of the country's inhabitants). The Northern district is the most sparsely populated, while the Eastern, Western and Southern districts are fairly evenly balanced. The largest river in the country runs from the northern mountains through Capitol City to the southern harbor. The rivers provide ample water for all sectors of the country, but are not navigable for their entire lengths.

Hypothetica has a long political history of independence from foreign intervention. For more than five hundred years the country was ruled by a succession of monarchs. It is now and has been since the 1930's a representative democracy comprised of a national parliament based on the five districts, ministers elected from each district based upon population. The principal administrator of the country is the prime minister, elected by members of parliament.

Further data concerning *Hypothetica* is found in each of the five district fact sheets.

About eight months ago, a team of Hypothetican geologists and University students discovered evidence of valuable mineral deposits in the northwest of Northern District. Further exploration by the Hypothetican government revealed the mineral deposit to be one of the richest and largest ever uncovered. The discovery has triggered great national excitement and, quite obviously, holds great potential for the future of *Hypothetica*. To that end, the prime minister has named a special national task force to assist with the compilation of a plan for the exploitation of the deposit and national development. Prior to calling a national conference of special district representatives, the prime minister has sent a draft of issues (proposals) to the five districts of his country. He has advised them to discuss the implications of the questions among themselves and to send two representatives (one to be the official spokesman, the other to act as liaison between the spokesman and his district) to the national conference at

Capitol City. The purpose of the conference will be to discuss the questions and exchange views on how best to proceed.

Problem

(Note: The instructor might choose any one or combination of the following problems, employed in any sequence, or invent one's own set of problems. The following are included here because they have been most commonly used in conducting this exercise.)

——What action should we take in regard to the discovery of the mineral deposit? What are the local and national considerations? What set of action steps should be followed and in what sequence?

——Given that the only feasible manner of transporting the ore from the deposit site to the harbor for export is by rail, we have obtained capital for the construction of a single-trunk main line between the two locations. What route should the railroad take? What are the justifications for that route? What are the implications?

——Foreign Mining Company has made a firm offer to develop the new mineral discovery. The company has also offered to pay a substantial royalty to the Hypothetican government on all minerals taken from the country. According to the latest assay reports, the Hypothetican treasury will grow phenomenally large, and the Foreign Mining Company has agreed to pay one-tenth of the total appraised worth of the deposit immediately upon delivery of signed agreements. The company has also offered to employ all Hypotheticans who wish to work in the mine as non-technical labor. Foreign Mining Company will supply management and technical personnel as well as non-technical workers should the local labor supply prove insufficient for satisfactory operation of the mine. What should be our country's response to Foreign Mining Company's offer?

——Develop a long-range plan for national development economically, educationally, and socially based upon a GNP that is ten times larger than that which currently exists in *Hypothetica*. This master plan should be developed taking into account all five districts of *Hypothetica* and aim to improve the standard of living in each consistent with differing life styles found in each state.

(There are, of course, a number of similar problems which can be developed to frame the exercise. In longer iterations of the exercise, the instructor may wish to write brief role descriptions for each participant that are consistent with the district in which they live, attempting to provide a range of behaviors. For example, in the Southern district, one participant might be made a boat owner, with seven years education, a family of six, serving as a minor elected official in South Center, earning $250 annually, etc.; while still another participant from Southern district might be styled as an illiterate fish packer, no formal education, earning $55 annually, married with a family of five, etc. During the exercise, such role players are asked to keep in mind their immediate and personal contexts in making contributions to the discussions.)

Hypothetica: The Northern District

1. *Population*—Hypothetica's most sparsely populated district (120,000), several small villages, one minor population center (4,000).
2. *Industry*—Lumber and forestry (limited), cordage, tanning and some leather goods.
3. *Education*—Meager facilities and little apparent interest.
4. *Transportation*—Mainly trails and one-lane dirt roads, one partially gravelled road used primarily for transportation of lumber to Capitol City. Two-day-a-week bus service to Capitol City from North Center (one round trip).
5. *Communication*—Generally good reception of HNR-1 radio from Capitol City. The vast majority of radio receivers are concentrated in North Center and larger villages. Monthly newspaper printed in North Center, but district's low literacy rate restricts circulation to under 3,000. Weekly mail service to North Center, sporadic delivery to outlying villages. Telephone service restricted to North Center, but inconsequential number of instruments available.
6. *Income.*   Annual per capita $110
   Daily   per capita   37¢   (310 days)
   Hourly per capita   3.7¢
   A hand saw costs approximately 40 cents
7. *Politics.* The district is administered by the District High Commissioner, elected by district commissioners, who themselves stand for election every two years. In addition, the Northern District elects 12 ministers to the national Parliament (one for every 10,000 population). A Northerner has never served as Prime Minister.

Hypothetica: The Eastern District

1. *Population.* Eastern District has a population of 425,000, well dispersed throughout the state. Its largest population area, East Center, has about 75,000 persons, a main processing and shipping point for farm products. There are two additional smaller population centers in the district serving the same function. The majority of the population lives in rural areas.
2. *Industry.* The district's main industry is agriculture. Main crops included corn, rice, barley, sugar beets, soy beans, hops. There is a developing dairy industry. Food processing for internal consumption and export. Exports consist of citrus fruits, soybeans, and specialized meat products.

3. *Education.* Schools are over-crowded and generally sub-standard for *Hypothetica.* There is one technical agricultural school in East Center.
4. *Transportation.* Generally very poor roads. One gravel road leads to Capitol city, used primarily for trucking grain and some pork. Three-day-a-week bus service to Capitol City. Sporadic barge traffic from Eastern District's northern population center to East Center.
5. *Communication.* Excellent reception of HNR-1 from Capitol City. A weekly newspaper is published in East Center and the agricultural school prints a very popular technical bulletin once a month. The Eastern District Government has an active extension program with agents making regular visits to the larger farms. Since most of the farming is of the tenant variety, many crop producers fail to benefit from the service. There are about 1,000 phones in the district, located primarily in East Center. Mail is delivered from Capitol City three times weekly, and the same schedule is maintained throughout the district, post office delivery only.
6. *Income.*   Annual per capita $120
   Daily   per capita   52¢   (310 days)
   Hourly per capita   5.2¢
7. *Politics.* The district is administered by the District High Commissioner, elected by district commissioners, who themselves stand for election every two years. In addition, the Eastern District elects 42 ministers to the national Parliament (one for every 10,000 population). An Easterner has never served as Prime Minister.

Hypothetica: The Southern District

1. *Population.* Hypothetica's second largest district (425,000), a little more a fourth of whom live in South Center (125,000). The harbor coast is heavily dotted with fishing villages, including South Island located at the mouth of the harbor.
2. *Industry.* Fishing and various related activities make up the bulk of industry in Southern District. While some fishermen build their own boats, this activity accounts for much of the District's economy. Salting, smoking and some canning of fish for both internal consumption and export account for an equally large share of the Southern District's economy. All imports and exports come and go through the harbor and South Center. Dock work, warehouses, and transportation provide additional opportunities for employment in the south.
3. *Education.* School system surpassed only by that of Central District. Good facilities, compulsory education through age fourteen. Good vocational school located in South Center.
4. *Transportation.* Hypothetica's "showcase" highway connects South Center with Capitol City 200 miles north. Exports and imports are

carried to and from Capitol City by truck. Five buses go to Capitol City and return each day. Dirt and partially gravelled roads link the district's many fishing villages. There is no scheduled transportation to South Island.

5. *Communication.* Excellent reception of HNR-1 radio from Capitol City, with some home radio programs emanating from South Center on a time-sharing basis with HNR-1. A daily newspaper is published in South Center, circulated mainly in the urban area. There are about 2000 telephones in the Southern District. There is one post office in each of the major villages for mail that goes to South Center and Capitol City.

6. *Income.*   Annual per capita $200
Daily   per capita   65¢   (310 days)
Hourly per capita   6.5¢
A fishing boat costs $500

7. *Politics.* The district is administered by the District High Commissioner, elected by district commissioners, who themselves stand for election every two years. In addition, Southern District elects 42 ministers to the national Parliament (one for every 10,000 population). One Southerner has served as Prime Minister since the representative form of government was established.

Hypothetica: The Western District

1. *Population.* Western District has a population of 400,000 distributed unevenly throughout the state. The district's population center is West Center with a population of 150,000. The district has fewer villages and towns than one might expect, because many of its citizens are nomadic, following their herds from place to place.

2. *Industry.* Major industries are meatpacking and woolen textiles. Tanning and dairy products exist to a lesser degree. Large ranches provide the bulk of beef and wool supporting the major industries, while little input to industry (except for a few animal hides for tanning) comes from the nomadic segment of the population.

3. *Education.* A wide range exists in educational programs. West Center has an excellent school system, including a two-year college with programs in animal husbandry. The rest of the district, however, has very poor schools where they do exist.

4. *Transportation.* A paved highway connects West Center with Capitol City only 70 miles away. There is twice daily bus service to the Capitol. West Center itself is second only to the Capitol in number of paved streets, and a number of paved roads join large ranches with West Center.

5. *Communication.* Excellent reception of HNR-1 radio from Capitol City with 90 per cent of the receivers concentrated in West Center. A

weekly newspaper is published in West Center with circulation confined to that city and several large ranches. The district as a whole has one of the country's lowest literacy rates. There is daily mail delivery to West Center and to private post offices on several large ranches. Occasional and irregular mail service elsewhere in the district. Telephone service is available in West Center and to large ranches, but nonexistent in other parts of the district.

6. *Income.* Some explanation of the Western District's economy is necessary because of its peculiar structure. The district is composed of a number of wealthy ranchers controlling hugh acreages in the central part of the district. It is this wealth and influence that has brought considerable benefits to West Center and its inhabitants. The bulk of the population of Western District, however, are extremely poor, rootless people, living from the land and their herds. Per capita figures would not accurately reflect the economic situation of Western District, so two averages are presented: one for West Center including ranchers, and one for the other two-thirds of the district's population.

West Center and Ranchers
Annual Average Income $550
Daily   Average Income $1.75   (310 days)
Hourly Average Income   17¢

Herders, Itinerate Farmers
Annual Average Income $50
Daily   Average Income 16¢
Hourly Average Income 1.6¢

7. *Politics.* The district is administered by the District High Commissioner, elected by District Commissioners, who themselves stand for election every two years. In addition, the Western District elects 40 ministers to the national Parliament (one for every 10,000 population). A number of Westerners have served as Hypothetica's Prime Minister over the years. The Western District has recently been experiencing some political unrest as a result of the activities of a group of young herders who resent the domination of the District Commission and seats in the national Parliament by ranchers. Through the young herders efforts, two ministers of Parliament from their group were elected last year and they won a small minority of seats on the District Commission.

Hypothetica: The Central District

1. *Population.* Nearly half of Hypothetica's population, 1,100,000 persons, live in the Central District. Capitol City has a population of 600,000, and the remainder of the inhabitants live in suburbs and towns surrounding the Capitol.

2. *Industry*. The district is the industrial hub of the country. Products and raw materials are shipped from every district for processing and manufacturing. Such industries include meatpacking and canning, flour mills, furniture making, distilling, food processing and canning, manufacturing of leather goods, woolen mills, clothing manufacturing, building materials and small tools. In addition, fuel distilleries and a large electrical plant provide the main sources of energy for the entire country. Government provides a large number of employment opportunities.

3. *Education*. A well developed school system, with compulsory education through the age of 14. The system includes two trade schools and the district is the site of Hypothetica University.

4. *Transportation*. Paved streets throughout the Capitol City and most outlying towns. Major paved highway to West Center and Hypothetica's "showcase" four lane highway linking Capitol City with South Center. Bus and electric tram transportation within Capitol City with additional transportation available from two private taxicab companies. Good bus transportation throughout the district. A large majority of the country's private automobiles are operated in the Central District. There are several private trucking firms and a large number of government and industrial vehicles in operation. One out of every ten families has a telephone, and nearly 70 per cent own radios. Capitol City is the base of operation for Hypothetica National Radio (100,000 watts) and its new television station (three hours of operation nightly), although few persons own TV sets. There are two daily newspapers, one privately owned and one government owned, both published in Capitol City. The privately owned newspaper also publishes several magazines. There is daily mail service in the district, delivered to addresses in Capitol City and to post offices in the suburbs and towns.

6. *Income*.   Annual per capita $450
             Daily   per capita $1.45
             Hourly per capita   14¢

7. *Politics*. The District is administered by the District High Commissioner, elected by District Commissioners, who themselves stand for election every two years. In addition, Central District elects 110 ministers to the national Parliament (one for every 10,000 population). The majority of Hypothetica's prime ministers have been from the Central District. The High Commissioner's post in the Central District has traditionally proved a jumping off postition for future prime ministers.

46. Communication and Social Integration

This game is designed to demonstrate some of the inter-relationships between communication and society through the creation and subsequent merging of two separate societies. One of the two societies (Society A) is provided tasks designed to bring about norms of integration, interdependence and cooperation, while the other (Society 1) is provided a context which fosters individualism, independence and competitiveness among its members. After the two societies have been established independently, Society 1 (a minority) is introduced to Society A with the intention of integrating the two. This exercise may be conducted with groups ranging from 15 to 50 participants, and requires approximately one hour.

Procedure:
1. Collect and assemble the following materials:
   a. Using poster board, construct 10 sets of Figure 46.1 for each participant in Society 1, and one set of Figure 46.2 for *every* participant taking part in the exercise.
   b. One envelope per participant.
   c. One die per each group in Society 1.
2. Divide the total group into two societies, Society 1 being about half the size of Society A.
3. Move the two societies into different rooms.
4. Seat the members of Society 1 around one table (if the group exceeds 15 members use two groups; Society 1 groups should be intentionally large). Tell the participants:
   "You are a member of a society in which you earn your livelihood by constructing 'T's.' These 'T's' must be formed using four triangles and three squares. You will take ordered turns in

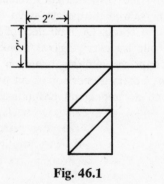

Fig. 46.1

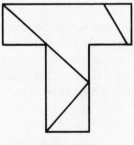

Fig. 46.2

acquiring the shapes following one of two options: a) you may upon your turn simply take any two pieces from the pile, or, b) you may choose to roll the die with the following possibilities: even number rolled (2, 4, 6), select that number of pieces,— odd number rolled (1, 3, 5), lose that number of pieces from those accumulated thus far, including those composing complete 'T's.' The member with the greatest number of 'T's' will be declared the wealthiest."

5. Place all of the pieces (enough for 10 complete "T's" per participant) in the center of Society 1's table(s).

6. Society 1 continues this activity until called upon to join Society A.

7. Meanwhile, a second instructor divides the members of Society A into groups of not larger than four to five members each, seating each group around a table separate from the other groups.

8. Tell the members of Society A they are to earn their livelihood by forming "T's", but do not instruct them how to construct the "T's."

9. Each member of Society A is to form one "T" using the five pieces as shown in Figure 46.2. To start the exercise for Society A, take one five-piece puzzle for each member of each small group, and randomly divide the pieces into as many envelopes as there are people (making sure that no one envelope contains the correct five pieces for completing a "T"). For example, if there is a four-member subgroup in Society A, four complete "T's" will be broken up, and from the resulting 20 pieces, five each will be randomly distributed into four envelopes. Give one closed envelope to each member of the subgroup and tell them to wait for further instructions. This process is repeated for as many subgroups as exist in Society A.

10. Instruct the group that there are enough pieces between the members of each subgroup to form one complete "T" for each member, and that no one member has the right combination of pieces to complete his or her "T."

11. Tell the group further that one of the things often lacking in the early stages of societal formation is a common language, therefore, the exercise will be conducted without any form of communication between members except as conforms to the following instructions:

"You must share pieces in order to be successful. You may offer pieces to other members of your group and accept pieces offered you by other members of your group, this offering being on a one-to-one basis only. There will be no common pool of offered pieces. You may *not* ask for pieces or take pieces not offered, nor may you indicate by pointing, talking, nudging, grimacing, etc., that you want a particular piece. In exchanging pieces simply hand them to the person you wish without demonstrating to him how the piece fits into his 'T'. You have five minutes to complete this task. You may open your envelopes."

12. After five minutes, collect each group's pieces and again place pieces randomly into their envelopes.
13. Tell participants they are now to begin a second round of "T" building except that this time they may use any form of communication they wish, but that all other rules remain in effect. Allow another five minutes for this activity.
14. At the end of five minutes, have members of successful groups help train members of less successful groups in "T" formation. After training, collect the pieces again.
15. At this point in the exercise, bring Society 1 into the room and evenly distribute them among Society A's groups. Add to each group's "T's" one additional "T" for each new member. Take the combined pieces and randomly distribute them into envelopes, one for each member of the integrated groups.
16. Read the following instructions:
    "The members of Society 1 are to be regarded as immigrants to Society A. They are to have a part in the work of the Society, and the sooner they learn how to earn a livelihood the better off the Society will be. There are some problems, however. Members of Society 1 do not speak Society A's language. Therefore, there will be no talking. And, as there is a possibility that gestures, pointing, taking pieces that are not clearly offered, and so on might be misinterpreted (pointing with the forefinger being a reflection on one's ancestry, etc.) there will be no gesturing, pointing, and so on."
17. In addition, tell the new members that they must again form "T's" but that the pieces are now different. With no further instructions, distribute the envelopes and tell participants to begin work. This part of the exercise may run as long as the instructor wishes, but probably should not be allowed to continue for more than ten minutes.

Discussion:

It is useful to begin the discussion by letting members of each society express their feelings about working in the integrated units. Members of Society A can be asked to explain to Society 1 members how their society was formed and vice-versa. Members of successful groups in the combined society can be asked to explain why they think they were successful, and unsuccessful groups speculate about their failure. Depending upon the goals of the exercise, the discussion can be led into a number of areas (societal formation, discrimination, integration, role and cultural assumptions, dissemination of knowledge) drawing specific references from participants' experiences in the exercise.

47. Political Communication

This game provides a context in which participants serve as reporters, sources and observers, and thereby gain a sense of the range of perspectives from which a single news event is viewed. The activity can be used with roughly 50 participants and requires two to four hours over several days.

The exercise consists of three phases: 1) the County Convention; 2) the State Convention; 3) Discussion Session. During the exercise, students have an opportunity to assume two of four possible roles. The available roles are: 1) County Convention Delegate; 2) State Convention Delegate; 3) Member of the Convention Gallery; and 4) Mass Media Reporter.

Procedure:

PHASE I

The participants are divided into two groups, half becoming convention delegates and the other half becoming mass media reporters.

County Convention Representatives: The representatives are divided into five equal groups. The groups are convened and each is given the task of arriving at a platform based on a number of issues suggested by the instructor prior to the beginning of the game.

County Convention Reporters: Reporters are divided into five equal groups. Each group has the task of covering one of the county conventions. Additionally, each group must prepare an article or series of articles providing an account of the convention they covered. These accounts are distributed to other game participants. Media reporters may cover the representatives' deliberations in any way they choose, utilizing the technologies of print, audio and video as available.

Approximately fifteen minutes should be allowed for the county conventions. At the conclusion of the first phase, each group of representatives selects two members of the convention to serve as delegates to represent their interests in the second stage of the game, at the *state convention.*

At the same time, each of the media groups produces a county convention report to be mass distributed. After completing their county convention reports, each medium selects two of its reporters to serve as correspondents to the state convention. The members of each group may be asked to choose their state correspondents on the basis of their ability to handle reportorial duties. However, the instructor may also suggest that each group choose correspondents on the basis of whatever criteria they can mutually arrive at after discussion among enterprise members.

PHASE 2

The second Phase of the game centers on the state convention. The delegates from each county that have been chosen to represent their respective counties meet to decide upon a state platform. The state correspondents arrive on the scene to report on the convention activity. And, the surplus of county delegates and mass media reporters converge upon the convention as "gallery." See Fig. 47.1.

State Convention Delegates: The task of the ten state delegates is to formulate a state-wide party platform, taking into account the decisions which have already been made at the county level.

State Convention Correspondents: The task of the team of correspondents is to cover the state convention and to prepare articles for distribution to the other game participants.

State Convention Observers: Those who are not chosen to participate as a delegate or correspondent serve as observers during the state convention, and later, will be called upon to make judgments as to the validity, accuracy, fairness and editorial balance exhibited in the stories or articles prepared and distributed by the correspondents.

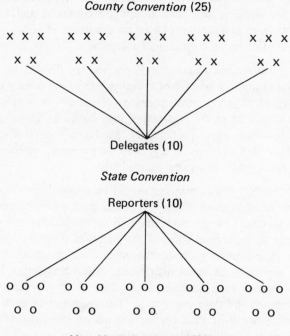

County Convention (25)

Delegates (10)

State Convention

Reporters (10)

Mass Media Enterprises (25)

Fig. 47.1

Roughly twenty minutes should be allowed for the state convention. However, this amount of time may be adjusted to be more appropriate with the time needed by other methods of news coverage (radio, taping, video-tape).

PHASE 3

The news stories and the articles prepared by the correspondents are then released to the delegates and observers and serve as the basis for discussing the adequacy of the reportorial activity at the two conventions.

Of greater importance is the opportunity this discussion provides for comparing the perceptions of news sources, reporters and observers, and for finer perceptual and judgmental differences which may come into play for individuals within each of those role categories.

In general, the function at this stage of the game is to encourage students to conceptually relate their experiences as participants in the game, to their own, and others' experiences in the "real world" examining differences and similarities and the implications for the understanding and improving of communication in a political context.

Discussion:

Where appropriate and desirable, the discussion exercise can also focus upon the elements of cooperation, persuasion, decision-making and the nature of political communication systems in general. Participants may also wish to explore the role of mass media in political communication processes. Do the media create or reflect public opinion? Discuss.

48. Mass Communication and the Pressbox

This game is designed to duplicate aspects of the sports reporting and writing processes within the classroom context, thereby allowing all participants to witness and report upon a "singular" event from a similar perspective. As such the activity affords the opportunity for participants to study the journalistic process and to compare their own perceptions and reports with others. The exercise requires from one to several hours and can be utilized with 10 to 40 participants.

Materials:

Any one of several sports table games, such as electric football, basketball or hockey.

Procedure:

1. Create hypothetical pre-game information sheets to be distributed to participants assigning names and numerals to players. Also create hypothetical season statistics on individual players and teams.
2. Divide the group into three subgroups. One group will serve as players and will operate the game. The second group will serve as reporters, and the third group will function as spectators. The number of individuals assigned to each role will, of course, vary depending upon the number of individuals and physical facilities involved and the particular game being used.
3. Provide all groups with pre-game hypothetical statistics, with instructions that they may be used in whatever manner the participants desire.
4. Begin game play. Instructors serve as time-keepers, referees and announcers.
5. Following the completion of game play, each reporter prepares a story which covers the game from his point of view.
6. These stories are duplicated and distributed to all participants for discussion.

Discussion:

Were there critical differences in the manner in which different reporters saw and/or reported the game? Were there similarities? Did the perceptions of the reporters differ from those of the spectators or players? If so, in what ways? Why? In what ways is this activity similar in nature to the process underlying the creation of news stories of all sorts? Are the problems similar? If so, what are the implications of this?

49. Communication System Simulation

The following simulation provides the basic framework necessary to create, maintain and elaborate an inter-related society of communicators and mass communicators. Working individually and in groups, in the context of co-operation and competition, it will be possible for participants to experience the dynamics of communication and mass communication and the role of these phenomena in individual and social organization. Participants serve in a series of several sequence roles, each of which has its own set of communicative demands, problems, and satisfactions. Some rules stress communicating-to and others being communicated-with. Many of the challenges and problems that will be encountered by a participant are virtually identical to those experienced in society at large.

This exercise is designed for 25 to 150 participants, and can be utilized for periods ranging from several hours to several semesters.

Procedure:

1. Form groups of 4 or 5 persons each.
2. The instructor selects a topic or topics to be researched and reported upon within a designated time period. If the exercise is planned to last a semester or longer, set up a production and evaluation schedule which lists the topics, project due dates, and evaluation due dates. For example:

Publication Period	Due Date (5:00 PM)	Evaluation Due Date (5:00 PM)
1 Research and report upon state election	Nov. 13	Nov. 15
2 Documentation of a current bill in the State Legislature hopper	Nov. 27	Nov. 29

3. Designate two-thirds of the groups as Freelance Agents. Designate the remaining one-third of the groups as Media Enterprise Editor/Managers. (If more than one production period is to be conducted, keep track of what groups play what roles, so roles can be rotated.)
4. Provide participants the following description:

Those of you serving as freelancers, will be preparing documentaries, stories, articles, and picture stories for the other members of the media community. In addition to working on message strategies and preparation, you will find yourselves in various interpersonal communication situations as you endeavor to sell your work to the participants who serve in the managerial capacities on mass media enterprises. As media enterprise editor/managers you will grapple with problems of interpersonal, group, and organization communication as you work to coordinate your enterprise with the goal of publishing a product, which meets the needs of your audience.

All of you will serve as members of the audience, and evaluate the publications of the various media enterprises after product distribution or presentation. In much the same way as subscribers evaluate newspapers, magazines, radio and television offerings, you will rate media enterprise products. These evaluations are converted to income points which are given to media enterprise managers to pay operating expenses, salaries of staff, freelancers' salaries and other expenses. The points you accumulate will be converted to grades at the close of the exercise.

5. Provide the following descriptions to appropriate participants.

Freelancers

The freelancer's objective is to conceive, plan, and consistently prepare messages of the highest possible quality to be published by one of the media enterprises.

Each freelancer is responsible for completion of the *Freelancer Contract Form* provided in Fig. 49.1 in *triplicate* promptly upon reaching an agreement. *One* copy to be retained by the *employing* enterprise, and *one copy must be submitted to the instructor.* The income must be specified on the contract and can in no way be contingent upon the evaluation the finished publication receives.

Each freelancer must complete and submit the *Publication Evaluation Form* provided in Fig. 49.2 to the instructor following the distribution of the finished products for each publication period.

Media Enterprise Editor/Managers

The editor/manager's objective is to conceive of, plan, prepare, produce and distribute an integrated publication of the highest possible quality and market value.

Each enterprise must complete two copies of the Media Enterprise Charter provided in Fig. 49.3. The completed forms must be submitted to the instructor. Any change in personnel must be submitted to the staff in writing.

Each enterprise which is operating during a publication period (one-third of groups formed) will contract 8–9 freelancers (or number designated so each publishing media enterprise will have approximately the same number of freelancers) per publication period.

Each enterprise will be responsible for the distribution of its publication to the entire community.

FREELANCE CONTRACT

Enterprise Name: _____

Freelancer Contracted: _____

Points Allocated: _____

Contract Applies for Publication Period: 1 2 3 4 5 6
      (Circle One)

Date Contract Begins: _____ Contract Termination Date: _____

Conditions Specified by this Contract: _____

_____

_____

_____

_____

_____

_____

_____

_____

_____

_____

I will comply with the above conditions:

    (Freelancer Signature)   (Date)

_____
(Enterprise Representative)   (Date)

Fig. 49.1

An editor/manager may resign from an enterprise if: (1) he can find an editor/manager who is willing to exchange positions with him, (2) the exchange is satisfactory to the other members of both enterprises.

Audience Evaluation

As an evaluating audience member, your objective is to rank the enterprise publications in terms of *your own assessment of their*

PUBLICATION EVALUATION FORM

Date _____

Name _____

Enterprise Name   Rank*
                                                                      (1-6)

_____

_____

_____

_____

_____

_____

_____

I verify that these rankings represent my independent and considered judgement.

Signature _____

_____

*Do not rank the enterprise with which you were affiliated during this publication period. Indicate your affiliation with an "X" in the rank column.

Fig. 49.2

adequacy. This suggests that each participant's evaluation will grow out of and reflect his own conception of what "adequacy" means to him.

All simulation participants will take part in the evaluation of the various publications of the community. The evaluation will be in the form of a rank-ordering of the enterprise products distributed at the end of each publication period.

The rules for ranking are: 1) Each member of the community will individually rank-order each of the products distributed, except the product of the enterprise with which he or she was affiliated for that period (as a freelancer or editor/manager). 2) The Publication Evaluation Form provided in Fig. 49.2 must be completed and submitted to the instructor within the specified time following the distribution of the publication.

MEDIA ENTERPRISE CHARTER

Date _____

Enterprise Name _____

Editorial/Managerial staff

Name	Local Address	Phone
_____	_____	_____
_____	_____	_____
_____	_____	_____
_____	_____	_____
_____	_____	_____
_____	_____	_____

_____
(Enterprise President)

Fig. 49.3

Discussion:

Discussion can be focused on many aspects of the simulation, some of which will arise naturally within the course of the exercise and be dealt with at that time. Further discussion can be directed towards: how problems developed and were dealt with by the various parties concerned; the development of community attitudes, norms, and rules; the factors of competition and cooperation in relation to inter and intra-group interactions, rationale and criteria used in product development and evaluation; the effects of that criteria on following production periods.

Bibliography

Allport, Gordon W., *Personality and Social Encounter,* Boston: Beacon House, 1960.

Bach, Robert C., *Communication,* New York: Hastings House, 1963.

Bagdikian, Ben H., *The Information Machines,* New York: Harper and Row, 1971.

Berger, Peter and Thomas Luckmann, *The Social Construction of Reality,* New York: Anchor, 1966.

Berlo, David K., *The Process of Communication,* New York: Holt, Rinehart and Winston, 1960.

Berrien, F. Kenneth, *General and Social Systems,* New Brunswick, N.J.: Rutgers University Press, 1969.

Bertalanffy, Ludwig von, *General System Theory,* New York: Braziller, 1968.

Blumer, Herbert, *Symbolic Interactionism,* Englewood Cliffs, N.J.: Prentice-Hall, 1969.

Bois, J. S., *The Art of Awareness,* Dubuque, Iowa: W. C. Brown, 1970.

Boulding, Kenneth, *The Image,* Ann Arbor: University of Michigan Press, 1960.

Boyd, Malcolm, *Crisis in Communication,* Garden City, N.Y.: Doubleday, 1957.

Brian, Russell, *The Nature of Experience,* Riddell Memorial Lectures, Oxford: Oxford University Press, 1959.

Brown, Roger W., *Words and Things,* New York: Free Press, 1958.

Britt, Stewart H., *Consumer Behavior and the Behavioral Sciences,* New York: Wiley, 1966.

Buckley, Walter, *Sociology and Modern Systems Theory,* Englewood Cliffs, N.J.: Prentice-Hall, 1967.

Budd, Richard W. and Brent D. Ruben, *Approaches to Human Communication,* Rochelle Park, N.J.: Hayden, 1972.

Burke, Kenneth, *Language as Symbolic Action,* Berkeley, Calif.: University of California Press, 1966.

Burke, Kenneth, *Permanence and Change,* New York: The New Republic, 1935.

Cantril, Hadley, *The Human Dimension,* New Brunswick, N.J.: Rutgers University Press, 1967.

Cantril, Hadley, *The Pattern of Human Concerns,* New Brunswick, N.J.: Rutgers University Press, 1965.

Carroll, John B., *Language and Thought,* Englewood Cliffs, N.J.: Prentice-Hall, 1964.

Casty, Alan, *Mass Media and Mass Man,* New York: Holt, Reinhart and Winston, 1968.

Church, J., *Language and the Discovery of Reality,* New York: Random House, 1961.

Churchman, C. West, *The Systems Approach,* New York: Dell, 1968.

Dance, Frank E. X., *Human Communication Theory,* New York: Holt Rinehart and Winston, 1967.

DeFleur, Melvin L., and Otto N. Larsen, *The Flow of Information,* New York: Harper, 1958.

DeFleur, Melvin L., *Theories of Mass Communication,* New York: David McKay, 1970.

Deutsch, Karl W., *Nationalism and Social Communication,* Cambridge, Mass.: M.I.T. Press, 1966.

Dexter, Lewis A., and David Manning White, *People, Society and Mass Communications,* New York: Free Press, 1964.

Dorsey, J. M. and W. H. Seegers, *Living Consciously,* Detroit: Wayne State Press, 1959.

Duncan, Hugh Dalziel, *Communication and Social Order,* New York: Oxford University Press, 1969.

Duncan, Hugh Dalziel, *Symbols and Social Theory,* New York: Oxford University Press, 1962.

Duncan, Hugh Dalziel, *Symbols in Society,* New York: Oxford University Press, 1968.

Efron, David, *Gesture and Environment,* New York: King's Crown Press, 1941.

Emery, Edwin, Phillip H. Ault, and Warren Agee, *Introduction to Mass Communications,* New York: Dodd, Mead, 1970.

Emery, Michael C. and Ted C. Smythe, *Readings in Mass Communications,* Dubuque, Iowa: W. C. Brown, 1972.

Fabun, Don, *Communications,* New York: Glencoe Press, 1971.

Fagen, Richard R., *Politics and Communication,* Boston: Little, Brown, 1966.

Farrar, Ronald T., and John D. Stevens, *Mass Media and the National Experience,* New York: Harper and Row, 1971.

Gerald, James E., *The Social Responsibility of the Press,* Minneapolis: University of Minnesota Press, 1963.

Gerth, Hans and C. Wright Mills, *Character and Social Structure,* New York: Harcourt, Brace, 1953.

Hall, Edward T., *The Hidden Dimension,* Garden City, N.Y.: Doubleday, 1966.

Haney, William V., *Communication and Organizational Behavior,* Homewood, Ill.: Richard D. Irwin, 1967.

Henle, Paul, *Language, Thought and Culture,* Ann Arbor: University of Michigan Press, 1959.

Herzberg, Frederick, et al., *The Motivation to Work,* New York: Wiley, 1959.

Hixson, Richard F., *Mass Media: A Casebook,* New York: Crowell, 1973.

Holzner, Burkart, *Reality Construction in Society,* Cambridge, Mass.: Schenkman, 1968.

Homans, G. C., *The Human Group,* New York: Harcourt, Brace, 1950.

Innis, Harold A., *The Bias of Communication,* Toronto: University of Toronto Press, 1951.

Kahn, Alfred J., *Neighborhood Information Centers,* New York: Columbia University School of Social Work, 1966.

Kelman, Herbert C., *International Behavior,* New York: Holt, Rinehart and Winston, 1965.

Klapper, Joseph T., *The Effects of Mass Communication,* Glencoe, Illinois: Free Press, 1961.

Knight, Frank H., *Risk, Uncertainty, and Profit,* Boston: Houghton Mifflin, 1921.

Korzybski, Alfred, *Science and Sanity,* Lakeville, Conn.: The International Non-Aristotelian Library Publishing Company, 1948.

Lacy, Dan M., *Freedom and Communications,* Urbana: University of Illinois Press, 1965.

Luft, Joseph, *Group Processes,* Palo Alto, Calif.: National Press, 1963.

Luft, Joseph, *Of Human Interaction,* Palo Alto, Calif.: National Press, 1971.

Machlup, Fritz, *The Production and Distribution of Knowledge in the United States,* Princeton, N.J.: Princeton University Press, 1962.

MacKay, Donald M., *Information, Mechanism, and Meaning,* Cambridge: M.I.T. Press, 1969.

Mann, Richard D. et al., *Interpersonal Style and Group Development,* New York: Wiley, 1967.

Matson, Floyd and Ashley Montagu, *The Human Dialogue,* New York: Free Press, 1967.

McLuhan, Marshall, *Understanding Media: The Extensions of Man,* New York: McGraw-Hill, 1964.

McLuhan, Marshall, *Verbi-voco-visual Explorations,* New York: Something Else Press, 1967.

McPhee, William N., *Formal Theories of Mass Behavior,* New York: Free Press, 1963.

Mendelbaum, Seymour J., *Community and Communications,* New York: W. W. Norton, 1972.

Merrill, John C. and Ralph L. Lowenstein, *Media, Messages and Men,* New York: David McKay, 1971.

Miller, Gerald and Michael Burgoon, *New Techniques in Persuasion,* New York: Harper and Row, 1972.

Monane, Joseph H., *A Sociology of Human Systems,* New York: Appleton-Century-Crofts, 1967.

Morris, Charles, *Signs, Language and Behavior,* New York: Braziller, 1946.

Mortensen, C. David, *Communication—The Study of Human Interaction,* New York: McGraw-Hill, 1972.

Nafziger, Ralph O. and David M. White, *Introduction to Mass Communications Research,* Baton Rouge: Louisiana State University Press, 1958.

Pepinsky, Harold B., *People and Information,* New York: Pergamon, 1970.

Peterson, Theodore, Jay W. Jensen, and William L. Rivers, *The Mass Media and Modern Society,* New York: Holt, Rinehart, and Winston, 1965.

Pike, Kenneth L., *Language in Relation to a Unified Theory of the Structure of Human Behavior,* The Hague: Mouton, 1967.

Riley, John W., Jr. and Matilda White Riley, "Mass Communication and the Social System," Robert K. Merton, Leonard Broom and Leonard S. Cottrell, Jr., *Sociology Today,* New York: Basic Books, 1959.

Rivers, William L. and Wilbur Schramm, *Responsibility in Mass Communication,* New York: Harper and Row, 1969.

Rogers, Everett M., *Communication of Innovations,* New York: Free Press, 1971.

Rosenberg, B. and David M. White, *Mass Culture Revisited,* New York: Van Nostrand, 1971.

Roslansky, John D., *Communication,* New York: Fleet Press, 1969.

Ruben, Brent D. and John Y. Kim, *Human Communication and General Systems Theory,* Rochelle Park, N.J.: Hayden, 1975.

Ruesch, Jurgen and Gregory Bateson, *Communication: The Social Matrix of Psychiatry,* New York: W. W. Norton, 1951, 1968.

Sackman, H. and Norman Nie, *The Information Utility and Social Choice,* Montvale, N.J.: American Federation of Information Processing Societies Press, 1970.

Schiller, Herbert I., *Mass Communications and the American Empire,* New York: Augustus Kelley, 1969.

Schramm, Wilbur, *Mass Communications,* Urbana, University of Illinois Press, 1960.

Schramm, Wilbur, *Mass Media and National Development,* Stanford: Stanford University Press, 1964.

Schramm, Wilbur, *Responsibility in Mass Communication,* New York: Harper, 1957.

Schramm, Wilbur, *The Process and Effects of Mass Communication,* Urbana: University of Illinois Press, 1954.

Sherif, Muzafer and Carl I. Hovland, *Social Judgment,* New Haven: Yale University Press, 1961.

Shibutani, Tamotsu, *Society and Personality,* Englewood Cliffs, N.J.: Prentice-Hall, 1961.

Siebert, Fredrick, Theodore Peterson and Wilbur Schramm, *Four Theories of the Press,* Urbana: University of Illinois Press, 1956.

Thayer, Lee, *Communication and Communication Systems,* Homewood, Ill.: Richard D. Irwin, 1968.

Thayer, Lee, *Communication, Theory and Research, International Symposium on Communication Theory and Research,* Springfield, Ill.: Thomas, 1967.

Tiger, Lionel, *Men in Groups,* New York: Random House, Vintage Books, 1969.

Vickers, Geoffrey, *Value Systems and Social Process,* New York: Basic Books, 1968.

Watzlawick, Paul, Janet H. Beavin and Don D. Jackson, *Pragmatics of Human Communication,* New York: W. W. Norton, 1967.

Whorf, B. L., *Language, Thought, and Reality,* Cambridge, Mass.: M.I.T. Press, 1956.

Wiener, N., *The Human Use of Human Beings,* New York: Avon, 1950.

Young, J. Z., *Doubt and Certainty in Science,* New York: Oxford University Press, 1950.

Part 4

COMMUNICATION OBSERVATION AND RECORDING GUIDES

Beyond actual participation in experience-based learning activities, a great deal can be learned about the dynamics of human communication by observing, describing, and analyzing social interaction from a semi-detached perspective. The guides in this section are designed to facilitate this kind of learning. Each form focuses its user's attention on particular aspects of the communication process, and will provide an important adjunct to the exercises, games, and simulations.

While the activity of observing and recording communication behavior is sometimes perceived by participants as less exciting than direct involvement in the simulations and games, the value of the role, both for the observer and the observed, clearly warrants its utilization. Rotating participants through both active participatory roles as well as the more detached observer and reporter function provides a maximally impactful and integrative learning experience. It is particularly desirable for observer reports to be fed into post-exercise discussions. In this manner, the observer feedback provides an additional point of view than the individuals who participated directly, and their reactions to the feedback will serve to help sharpen the observational and descriptive skills of the observer.

Observers will find it useful to distinguish between the *content of communication* and the *process of communication*. Content refers to what is being talked about—the subject of discussion. It is, of course, the dimension with which participants will be most familiar. Topical outlines, who says what to whom and in what order, storyline and plot have been experiences common to most students.

The process of communication is likely to be a much less familiar, far more subtle, and difficult to grasp concept for observers. It deals not with what is discussed, but rather *how* it is discussed. Process analysis focuses on the dynamics of leadership, levels of participation, modes of decision-making, patterns of influence, modes of verbal and nonverbal contribution, and so on.

One particularly useful approach to process observation is the "group-on-group" design. This consists of one group of individuals who participate directly in a decision-making or problem-solving activity, and an outer group of participants—ideally of an equal number—who observe the operating group's activity. The "Group Communication Observation Form" (Number 4), is well suited for this situation. After the activity group has completed its task, the observers lead a discussion of the processes of interaction they noted, using the descriptions and observations as the initial impetus.

A variation of this pattern is to have each individual in the task group observed by one, preselected individual from the observation group. The "Interpersonal Communication Observation Form" (Number 10), is useful for this design. Following the decision-making or problem-solving activity by the work group, the observer and the person he or she observed are paired for a five minute feedback and discussion session. The observer describes the communication behaviors of the person observed. As a part of the discussion, the observed individual may also share his own perceptions of his behaviors, which in some instances may differ markedly from those noted by his observer. In such instances, the more specific the description the observer can provide of the communication behavior of the individual observed, the more likely the information is to be useful to its receiver. Form 11, "Guidelines for Providing Useful Feedback" suggests additional guidelines.

Observers should be cautioned that in all cases their role is to describe communication behavior, not to judge or evaluate it as "good" or "bad," nor to attempt to explain why certain behaviors occurred. Following paired discussions, it is often useful to reunite the two original groups—workers and observers—to briefly discuss the group processes that were noted. This provides observers the opportunity to share their more general observations with the entire group, and often facilitates discussion of leadership, effects of leadership, group climate, directionality of information flow, and so on. If time permits, the instructor may wish to repeat the exercise reversing the roles of the groups.

Where conditions permit, video taping of many of the exercises in this volume will prove a powerful and valuable expansion of the process observation concept. Where replay of the tape is accompanied by discussion, participants have the opportunity to gain a quite different perspective on their own communication behavior.

1. Descriptions of Common Roles in Interpersonal and Group Communication

The following description of common roles in groups can be used as a basis for observing behavior in interpersonal and small group communication situations. Typically no one individual serves only in a single role, rather he or she may move in and out of several of these roles within a short period of time. These categories should therefore be looked upon as descriptions of particular modes of behavior, rather than of people.

A. Task Oriented Roles:

Facilitation and coordination of group problem solving activities.

1. Initiator:
   Offers new ideas or changed ways of regarding group problems or goals. Suggests solutions. How to handle group difficulty. New procedure for group. New organization for group.
2. Information seeker:
   Seeks clarification of suggestions in terms of factual adequacy and/or authoritative information and pertinent facts.
3. Information giver:
   Offers facts or generalizations which are "authoritative" or relates own experience pertinently to group problem.
4. Coordinator:
   Clarifies relationships among ideas and suggestions, pulls ideas and suggestions together, or tries to coordinate activities of members of sub-groups.
5. Evaluator:
   Subjects accomplishment of group to "standards" of group functioning. May evaluate or question "practicability," "logic," "facts," or "procedure" of a suggestion or of some unit of group discussion.

B. Relation Oriented Roles:

Building group-centered attitudes and orientation.

6. Encourager:
   Praises, agrees with, and accepts others' ideas. Indicates warmth and solidarity in his attitude toward members.
7. Harmonizer:
   Mediates intra-group scraps. Relieves tensions.
8. Gatekeeper:
   Encourages and facilitates participation of others. "Let's hear . . ." "Why not limit length of contributions so all can react to problem?"

9. Standard setter:
   Expresses standards for group to attempt to achieve in its functioning or applies standards in evaluating the quality of group processes. Raises questions of group goals and purpose and assesses group movement in light of those objectives.
10. Follower:
   Goes along somewhat passively. Provides friendly audience.
11. Group-observer:
   Stays out of group's proceedings; functions by giving feedback as to what goes on during various phases of the meeting.

C. Self-Oriented Roles:

   Tries to meet felt individual needs often at the expense of group.
12. Blocker:
   Negativistic. Stubbornly and unreasoningly resistant. Tries to bring back issue group intentionally rejected or by-passed.
13. Recognition-seeker:
   Tries to call attention to himself. May boast, report on personal achievements, and in unusual ways, struggles to prevent being placed in "inferior" position, etc.
14. Dominator:
   Tries to assert authority in manipulating group or some individuals in group. May be flattery, assertion of superior status or right to attention, giving directions authoritatively, interrupting contributions of others, etc.
15. Avoider:
   Maintains distance from others. Passive resister. Tries to remain insulated from interaction.

2. Role Behavior Recording Form

Study the role descriptions provided in Form 1. Then for each group member place a check in the column corresponding to the role most often filled by each.

Group Members

Roles

	A	B	C	D	E	F	G	H	I	J	K	L	M	N
1. Initiator Contributor														
2. Information Seeker														
3. Information Giver														
4. Coordinator														
5. Evaluator														
6. Encourager														
7. Harmonizer														
8. Gatekeeper														
9. Standard Setter														
10. Follower														
11. Group Observer														
12. Blocker														
13. Recognition Seeker														
14. Dominator														
15. Avoider														

3. Interpersonal and Small Group Role Description Form

This form provides an alternative manner for recording functional roles within a group. It is designed for one-on-one observation.

Work Roles	Never	Seldom	Often	Frequently
1. Initiates ideas or actions	1	2	3	4
2. Facilitates introduction of facts and information	1	2	3	4
3. Clarifies issues	1	2	3	4
4. Evaluates	1	2	3	4
5. Summarizes and pulls together various ideas	1	2	3	4
6. Keeps the group working on the task	1	2	3	4
7. Consensus taker—asks to see if group is near decision	1	2	3	4
8. Requests further information	1	2	3	4

Participation Maintenance Roles				
1. Supports, encourages others	1	2	3	4
2. Reduces tension	1	2	3	4
3. Harmonizer—keeps peace	1	2	3	4
4. Compromiser—finds common ground	1	2	3	4
5. Encourages participation	1	2	3	4

Blocker Roles				
1. Expresses hostility	1	2	3	4
2. Seeks recognition	1	2	3	4
3. Avoids involvement	1	2	3	4
4. Dominates group	1	2	3	4
5. Nitpicks	1	2	3	4

4. Group Communication Observation Form

This form provides a basic framework for observing, recording and studying some elements of the communication dynamics which operate in small group interaction.

Interpersonal Communication

1. Expressing (verbal and non-verbal)

2. Listening

3. Responding

Communication Pattern

1. Directionality (one-to-one, one-to-group, all through a leader)

2. Content (thoughts, feelings, etc.)

3. Influence (who talks to whom, who looks at whom for support?)

Major Roles*

_____ Initiator   _____ Gatekeeper

_____ Information Seeker   _____ Standard Setter

_____ Information Giver   _____ Follower

_____ Coordinator   _____ Observer

_____ Evaluator   _____ Blocker

_____ Encourager   _____ Recognition Seeker

_____ Harmonizer   _____ Dominator

*Role descriptions provided in Form 1.

Leadership Style

1. Was the main leadership pattern democratic?

2. Was the main leadership pattern dictatorial?

3. Did a "do your own thing" leadership style prevail?

Effects of Leadership

1. Was participation generally good?

2. Was there a lack of enthusiasm by participants?

3. Did commitment seem low?

4. Were some participants holding back?

Participation

1. Who were the most active participators? Which participants were not active?

2. Were there major shifts in levels of participation during the activity?

3. How were low participators treated? How was their silence interpreted?

Influence

1. Who were the most influential members in the group? Who were the least influential?

2. Were there major shifts in sources of influence during the activity?

3. How many suggestions were rejected?

Decision Making

1. How were decisions made? By voting? Consensus? Ramrodding?

2. How focused was the group on its main topic of concern?

3. Were there particular clusters of group participants who would usually support one another in arriving at decisions? Were there groups or individuals who were frequently in conflict with one another?

4. How involved were all group members in arriving at decisions?

5. How did the group resolve major differences of opinion?

Norms

1. Were there certain topics which were generally avoided by the group (for example, religion, race, feelings for one another, sex, points of disagreement, etc.)?

2. Did members of the group conduct themselves in particularly polite or formal ways? Were members conducting themselves in a manner that seemed especially informal?

3. Were individual's feelings dealt with openly?

4. Were individual's motives dealt with openly?

Goals

1. Were group goals discussed?

2. Were the goals agreed upon?

3. Did the group accommodate diverse member goals?

Cohesion

1. Did group members tend to perceive situations similarly?

2. Did membership in the group provide interpersonal rewards?

Group Climate

1. How would you characterize the general climate of the group?

2. Did members of the group seem to have sincere regard for one another's thoughts and feelings?

Situational Factors

1. What were the effects of the group size?

2. Was time a factor in the group's process?

3. Were physical facilities an important factor in determining the nature of interaction (for example, seating arrangement, tables, etc.)?

4. Were all members present for entire interaction?

5. Recording Information Networks

Observing message flows within a group can be useful for studying and reporting upon such factors of group communication as influence, status, interpersonal attraction, participation, attention, etc.

Procedure:

1. Record the order of speakers, either directly as the meeting progresses or from tape recordings afterward.
2. Pictorially depict message flow pattern as follows:
   a) draw a circle using group members' names or initials as points along its circumference as in Fig. 5.1

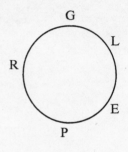

Fig. 5.1

b) Indicate message initiation by drawing lines from the first speaker to the next to the next and so on; where overlapping occurs, curve lines slightly so they will be apparent. (i.e. Record—Ron, Gayle, Ron, Pat, Ed, Lynn, Ron . . . as in Fig. 5.2.

Fig. 5.2

6. Small Group Interaction Content Guide

In group meetings, especially those of a task-oriented nature, it is, of course, desirable for a major portion of the discussions to remain on the subject at hand. Group members are often unaware of straying from the topic. This guide suggests a means of studying and reporting on a group's topical patterns.

Instructions:

1. Using audio or video tape recorder, record a group discussion.
2. Transcribe individual's statements onto paper.
3. Categorize each statement, starting with the first as either on the subject or off the subject. (For these purposes "on the subject" can be defined in one of two ways: 1) using the first statement of the session as the establishment of the subject, or 2) using the first statement that directs the group's attention to the task or task-related matter as the subject topic.)
4. Develop a table, entering group members' names vertically and the two categories: "on-the-topic" and "off-the-topic" horizontally as in Fig. 6.1. Note: where desirable the table may be presented without indicating the names of individuals.

	on-topic	off-topic
Ed	𝍦𝍦	//
Gayle	/	
Pete	𝍦𝍦 𝍦𝍦	

Fig. 6.1

5. Place a tally-mark for each section of conversation in the section corresponding to the names of the speaker as shown in Fig. 6.1 When complete the result will provide a useful individual and group profile.

7. Intra-Group Perception Guide

The following method of observation involves direct questioning of group members in order to visually display some of the underlying patterns or relationships operating within a group. Patterns can be developed to explore a variety of dimensions, such as "who feels closest to whom within the group", "who do you consider to be the leader in the group," or "who looks to whom for negative feedback," etc.

Procedure:

1. Select the basis upon which a sociogram is to be constructed and develop a question or questions to get at the matters of concern.
2. At a session where *all* members can be asked the same questions at the same time, read off questions asking each member to respond in writing indicating one other group member's name. (i.e. Who do you feel closest to?—Ron)
3. After questions and answers are completed collect answer-sheets from each participant, making sure he or she has put his or her name on the paper as well.
4. To construct the sociogram, use one piece of paper for each question. Arrange members' names in circular order on the page, as in Fig. 7.1.

Ron

Ed

Ralph

Lynn

Gayle   **Fig. 7.1**

5. Record answers by drawing lines from name of person answering to the person indicated as in Fig. 7.2.

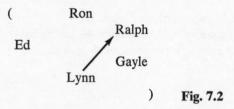

Follow this procedure until all members have an arrow from their name to the person indicated. Continue until all questions have been displayed in this manner.

6. Clearly, any number of patterns may appear, for example if no one indicates a particular person for an answer, that person can be diagrammatically depicted as an isolate as in Fig. 7.3.

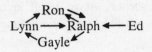

Fig. 7.3   (Here Ed might be considered an isolate.)

If one person is chosen by an overwhelming majority of responses, that can be diagrammatically depicted as a star structure as in fig. 7.4.

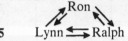

Fig. 7.4   Gayle

Often in larger groups subgroups may be in evidence. They can be depicted as a triangle as in Fig. 7.5.

Fig. 7.5

8. Verbal Interaction Recording Guide

This method of process observation involves recording the duration of verbal interaction and silences. It is useful in observing and recording patterns of participation and sequences of conversation flow.

Procedure:

1. Develop a table entering group members' names vertically and time sequences in units of 15 seconds each, horizontally.
2. Either by recording directly during meeting or by transcribing from tape recorder after the meeting, measure how long a person speaks and place a horizontal jagged line corresponding to the amount of time used, on the line that corresponds to the speaker.

	15 secs	30 secs	45 secs	1 min	1:15	1:30
Ed	∿∿∿∿∿∿∿∿					
Gayle						
Pete						

Fig. 8.1

Fig. 8.1 would indicate that Ed spoke for approximately 40 seconds.

3. To indicate that someone else continued the conversation immediately after the previous speaker stopped, draw a straight vertical line from the jagged line of the last speaker's name to the succeeding speaker at the same time unit on the table as in Fig. 8.2.

	15 secs	30 secs	45 secs	1 min	1:15	1:30
Ed	∿∿∿∿∿∿∿					
Gayle			∿∿∿∿			
Pete						

Fig. 8.2

Fig. 8.2 indicates Gayle has continued the conversation without a break occuring between the two speakers.

4. To indicate that there was a silence between speakers, a slanted straight line from the jagged line of the last speaker is drawn to the following speaker's area indicating the time spent in silence, as shown in Fig. 8.3

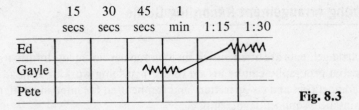

Fig. 8.3

This slanted line indicates a silent period of 15 seconds before Ed spoke after Gayle.

9. Seating Arrangement Recording Guide

Seating arrangements are often important to group development. Information about spatial geography can be an aid in distinguishing working conditions such as competition and co-operation, and can be used for inferring patterns of acquaintance, support, leadership, etc.

Procedure:

1. Keep a running record of where group members choose to sit by placing x's and group members' names in corresponding locations on paper as shown in Fig. 9.1.

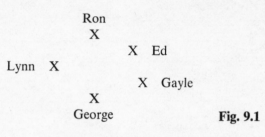

Fig. 9.1

2. If physical barriers are present, place them in the diagram as well as in Fig. 9.2.

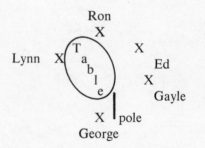

Fig. 9.2

3. If possible, take notes on type of meeting, noting any corresponding changes in discussion and seating arrangements. (Three major patterns emerging in group message networks can be identified: The chain depicting two-way interactions between all members except for the people at the extreme ends.

G ⟷ R ⟷ P ⟷ L ⟷ E   Fig. 9.3

The circle (Fig. 9.4) depicting a situation where every member speaks to two other members.

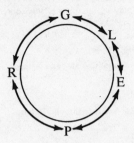

Fig. 9.4

The wheel (Fig. 9.5) depicting one person to which all statements are directed.

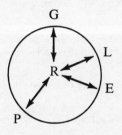

Fig. 9.5

10. Interpersonal Communication Observation Form

This form provides a basic framework for observing, recording, and reporting upon aspects of interpersonal communication. It is by no means a complete listing of the elements of interaction, and serves only as a summary of some observable elements of interpersonal dynamics.

Interpersonal Communication

1. Clarity of expression of thoughts and feelings

    a. Verbal
    b. Non-verbal

2. Range of expression of thoughts and feelings

    a. Verbal
    b. Non-verbal

3. Listens to the thoughts and feelings of others

General Orientation Categories

1. Task Orientation—Places primary emphasis on completing the task. Shows relatively less concern for the needs, feelings, and concerns of persons involved.

2. Intrapersonal Orientation—Places primary emphasis on his or her own needs, feelings, and concerns. Shows relatively less concern for the completion of the task itself or for the other persons.

3. Interpersonal Orientation—Places primary emphasis on the needs, feelings, and concerns of members other than himself. Shows relatively less concern for the completion of the task itself or for his own needs, feelings, and concerns.

Roles* in which the person observed functioned (where possible give examples).

* Role descriptions provided in Form 1.

11. Guidelines for Providing Useful Feedback

Feedback is communication to a person (or a group) which tells how he affects others. It can serve as a basis for the individual to correct his communication strategies to enhance the likelihood that the outcomes of his communicating will match his intentions.

Some criteria for useful feedback:

1. It is descriptive rather than evaluative. By describing one's own reaction, it leaves the individual free to use it or not to use it as he sees fit. By avoiding evaluative language, it reduces the need for the individual to respond defensively.

2. It is specific rather than general. To be told that one is "dominating" will probably not be as useful as to be told that "just now when we were deciding the issue, you did not appear to listen to what others said and I felt forced to accept your arguments or face attack from you."

3. It takes into account the needs of both the receiver and giver of feedback. Feedback can be destructive when it serves only our own needs and fails to consider the needs of the person on the receiving end.

4. It is directed toward behavior which the receiver can do something about. Frustration is only increased when a person is reminded of some shortcoming over which he has no control.

5. It is solicited, rather than imposed. Feedback is most useful when the receiver himself has formulated the kind of question which those observing him can answer.

6. It is well-timed. In general, feedback is most useful at the earliest opportunity after the given behavior (depending, of course, on the person's readiness to hear it, validation available from others, etc.)

7. It is checked to insure clarity. One way of doing this is to have the receiver try to rephrase the feedback he has received to see if it corresponds to what the sender had in mind.

8. When possible, check accuracy of the feedback with others in the group. Is this only one person's impression or an impression shared by others?

12. Barriers to Communication

The following check list of common barriers and impediments to communication may be useful in thinking about, identifying, and reporting on problems which arise during interpersonal, small group, and organizational interaction occuring as a part of games and simulations provided in this volume.

1. ____ Speaker seems to lack adequate knowledge of the subject or is insufficiently prepared.

2. ____ Speaker does not seem to believe in the message or the policy behind it.

3. ____ Receiver has inadequate knowledge of the subject or is inadequately prepared.

4. ____ Receiver is not interested in subject.

5. ____ Speaker or receiver is temporarily preoccupied with something else.

6. ____ Failure of people to say what they mean.

7. ____ Speaker and receiver have very different vocabularies.

8. ____ Racial differences between communicators.

9. ____ Age differences between communicators.

10. ____ Communicators have differing assumptions.

11. ____ Grade or status differences between communicators, (e.g. instructor-student).

12. ____ One of the communicators has negative or hostile reactions to the other.

13. ____ One of the communicators tends to be a "yes man" to the other.

14. ____ One or both parties is intentionally miscommunicating.

15. ____ Outside interference or distraction.

16. ____ Pressure of time.

17. ____ Inadequacy of words to express difficult ideas, thoughts, or situations.

18. ____ Same words have different meanings.

19. ____ Space and distance; lack of face-to-face contact.

20. ____ Gaps in formal communication system.

21. ____ Inadequate "feedback."

22. ____ _____

23. ____ _____

13. Intra-Group Evaluation Form

This form provides members of a group with a method for exploring their perceptions of the group's functioning.

Directions: In front of each of the items below there is a blank space. Rate your group on each characteristic using a seven-point scale, where 7 is "very much" and 1 is "very little."

Climate

_____ 1. I am treated as a human being rather than just another group member.

_____ 2. I feel close to the members of this group.

_____ 3. There is cooperation and teamwork present in this group.

_____ 4. Membership in this group is aiding my personal growth development.

_____ 5. I have trust and confidence in the other members of the group.

_____ 6. Members of this group display supportive behavior toward each other.

_____ 7. I derive satisfaction as a result of my membership in this group.

_____ 8. I feel psychologically close to this group.

_____ 9. I get a sense of accomplishment as a result of membership in this group.

_____ 10. I feel I can be honest in responding to this evaluation.

Data Flow

_____ 11. I am willing to share information with other members of the group.

_____ 12. I feel free to discuss important personal matters with group members.

_____ 13. I feel that I am oriented toward personal goals rather than toward helping the group achieve its objective.

_____ 14. This group uses integrative, constructive methods in problem-solving rather than a win-lose approach.

_____ 15. As a member of this group, I feel I am able to deal promptly and effectively with important group problems.

_____ 16. The activities of this group reflect a constructive integration of the needs and desires of its members.

_____ 17. My needs and desires are reflected in the activities of this group.

Control

_____ 18. I feel that there is a sense of real group responsibility for getting a job done.

_____ 19. I feel manipulated by the group.

_____ 20. I feel that I manipulate the group.

14. Group Climate Inventory

This form provides group members with a method for describing the climate of the group as they see it.

Directions: Think about how your fellow group members normally behave toward you. In the parentheses in front of the items below place the number corresponding to your perceptions of the group as a whole, using the following scale.

5 They can <u>always</u> be counted on to behave this way.
4 <u>Typically</u> I would expect them to behave this way.
3 I would <u>usually</u> expect them to behave this way.
2 They would <u>seldom</u> behave this way.
1 They would <u>rarely</u> behave this way.
0 I would <u>never</u> expect them to behave this way.

I would expect my fellow group members to:

1. (___) . . . . level with me.

2. . . . . . (___) . . . . get the drift of what I am trying to say.

3. . . . . (___) . . . . interrupt or ignore my comments.

4. . . . . (___) accept me for what I am.

5. (___) . . . . feel free to let me know when I "bug" them.

6. . . . . . (___) . . . . misconstrue things I say or do.

7. . . . . (___) . . . . be interested in me.

8. . . . . (___) provide an atmosphere where I can be myself.

9. (___) . . . . keep things to themselves to spare my feelings.

10. . . . . . (___) . . . . perceive what kind of person I really am.

11. . . . . (___) . . . . include me in what's going on.

12. . . . . (___) act "judgemental" with me.

13. (___) . . . . be completely frank with me.

14. . . . . . (___) . . . . recognize readily when something is bothering me.

15. . . . . (___) . . . . respect me as a person, apart from my skills or status.

16. . . . . (___) ridicule me or disapprove if I show my peculiarities.

(___) Genuineness
   (___) Understanding
      (___) Valuing
         (___) Acceptance

15. Personal and Group Meeting Reaction Form

This form provides group members with a method for describing and reporting their reactions to group or organizational meetings. Directions: Below are two sets of statements. You are to rank order the items in each set from 1, Most Like, to 10, Least Like, to characterize what the meeting was like. Use this procedure: rank 1 first, then 10, then 2, then 9, alternating toward the middle.

The meeting was like this:

(   ) There was much warmth and friendliness.

(   ) There was a lot of aggressive behavior.

(   ) People were uninterested and uninvolved.

(   ) People tried to dominate and take over.

(   ) We were in need of help.

(   ) Much of the conversation was irrelevant.

(   ) We were strictly task-oriented.

(   ) The members were being very polite.

(   ) There was a lot of underlying irritation.

(   ) We worked on our process problems.

My behavior was like this:

(   ) I was warm and friendly to some.

(   ) I did not participate much.

(   ) I concentrated on the job.

(   ) I tried to get everyone involved.

(   ) I took over the leadership.

(   ) I was polite to all the members.

(   ) My suggestions were frequently off the point.

(   ) I was a follower.

(   ) I was irritated.

(   ) I was eager and aggressive.

16. Individual and Group Climate Guide

The purpose of this exercise is to foster an examination of individual and group mood and changes in mood during group proceedings. The exercise is designed for use with small groups and requires 30 minutes to several hours.

Procedure:

1. Before the activity, prepare 40–50 oak tag or cardboard signs with yarn or string to hang around participants' necks, lettered with the words "I FEEL" and one word describing a particular feeling. A sample of such descriptive words follows:

confident	ambitious	silly
humorous	dynamic	humorless
unhappy	sensitive	accepted
extroverted	scared	mean
open	bored	isolated
quiet	detached	bizarre
motivated	cooperative	friendly
unfriendly	happy	useful
withdrawn	misunderstood	pushy
nervous	rejected	talkative
uncooperative	closed	insensitive
romantic	tense	helpful
observant	ecstatic	introverted
hungry	insecure	tired
frustrated	distracted	obnoxious

2. Arrange signs in a visible location.
3. Have participants think about how they feel at that moment and ask them to choose a sign that represents that feeling and hang it around their neck.
4. Have group proceed in its normal discussions.
5. Remind participants that as the discussion proceeds, their feelings might change and to, therefore, change feeling tags.

Discussion:

What reactions did participants have to the signs? How did the signs affect the group process? Were the signs helpful in your recognition of emotions? Why or why not? How? Did the signs have an effect on members' participation rates? What is the relevance of this exercise for everyday communication situations?